Complementary essays can be found in this section. For the proper introduction and Passover Haggadah, open from the opposite cover.

SLAVERY AND FREEDOM

Nothing is more central to the story of the Exodus than the contrast between Avdut and Herut, slavery and freedom. The liberation from bondage was such a foundational experience for the Jewish people that it pervades the prayers and provides the rationale for numerous Mitzvot.

How does Judaism define freedom? When I asked students which Harry Potter character best understood the concept of freedom, frankly, I was expecting them to say Dobby because he was freed by Harry and prided himself on being a free elf, a title which eventually became his epitaph. I expected them to answer Harry because he freed Dobby, or Hermione because she founded the Society for the Promotion of Elfish Welfare (S.P.E.W.), or even Sirius who reclaimed his freedom from Azkaban. While many did, indeed, choose those characters, others surprised me.

Some chose Dumbledore, or even Voldemort because they "could do whatever they wanted." To these students, power is freedom. They overlooked an important teaching of Judaism. The Rabbis say in *Ethics of the Fathers* that the truly free individual is the one who is engaged in the study of Torah. In other words, we do not see freedom as an abstract state, but as an opportunity to dedicate ourselves to a noble cause. We don't express the concept as "free-

THE
(unofficial)
HOGWARTS
HAGGADAH

MOSHE ROSENBERG

ISBN 9780692859056

90000 >

9 780692 859056

dom from," but as "freedom for." When the Israelites were redeemed from Egypt, they were "freed," but only when they received the Torah three months later were they truly "free." Seen through this prism, Dumbledore may have understood freedom not because of his power, but because he knew what to do with it. And Voldemort, enslaved as he was to hatred, drunk on power, was anything but free.

Still other students chose Fred and George Weasley, arguing that they lived life on their own terms, bucking conventional wisdom and expectations, and pursuing the dream of their store in Diagon Alley, despite discouragement from those around them. Clearly we, the readers, are meant to approve of their behavior, just as Harry does. In fact, Judaism has a streak of approval for the iconoclast who rejects the assumptions of the age. After all what was Abraham but just such a person, who taught monotheism to a polytheistic world? The *midrash* explains Abraham's descriptive: *Ha-Ivri* (the Hebrew, literally, the one from the "ever," side or riverbank) as meaning that the entire world of his time was on one side, while Abraham was on the other. Nevertheless, each society and religion ultimately do insist on a degree of conformity, and people who take non-conformity to an extreme can become slaves to the image they wish to project. For more on rule-breaking in Harry Potter and Judaism, you might want to read chapter 1 of *Morality for Muggles*.

As the definition of freedom is not simple, neither is the definition of slavery. Not all slavery is of the brick and mortar variety. Just as society has come to understand the ways in

which we enslave ourselves to substances or psychologically chain ourselves to harmful ideas, Judaism recognizes the many ways that human beings can give up their freedom to choose. The Book of Proverbs (22:7) declares, "The borrower is an *eved* to the lender," showing how financial obligation carries with it compromise of our freedom to choose and decide. The many verses that deal with those who are addicted to food and drink highlight the extent to which physical pleasure can be a taskmaster of the soul. But perhaps the most merciless slavedriver of all is the lust for power, personified in the Biblical characters of Haman and Pharaoh.

In the Book of Esther, Haman is the arch-manipulator, who seeks to destroy the Jewish people on his way to what he hopes will be the throne of Persia. He manipulates King Ahasuerus into issuing the decree for the Jews' extermination, no doubt thinking himself clever in his exploitation of the King's insecurities. But he is blinded to his own transparent hunger for power and is outflanked by Esther, who uses it against him. Ultimately, the King himself sees through his chief advisor. According to Rabbi Joseph B. Soloveitchik, on the fateful night when "the King could not sleep," he asks Haman how to reward the person whom the King wishes to honor, knowing that Haman will think that the honor is meant for him and reveal his true aims. Haman promptly takes the bait and asks to paraded around town dressed as the King, thus incriminating himself and beginning his downfall.

Rabbi David Silber in his Im L'Et Ka-Zot (Maggid, 2017), draws a fascinating contrast between the King and Haman which underscores just how far Haman had become enslaved to his baser emotions. Both characters are described as being filled with anger. In fact, the King is described three separate times as waxing wrathful. But each time that Ahasuerus is satisfied on the issue that provoked him, be it the disobedience of Queen Vashti or the insolence of Haman, the verse records that his anger subsided. Haman, on the other hand, is described as angry, but never portrayed as calming down. His anger is of the sort that does not lend itself to control, cannot be tamped back. Haman is in the hands of his own hubris. The *midrash* sums this up by saying, "The heart of the righteous is in their hands, while the wicked are in the hands of their heart."

No one better epitomizes the way we can enslave ourselves to our negative natures than Pharaoh. At the start of the Exodus narrative he is a free agent, able to choose to furlough the Israelites or hold onto them. Before the plagues of blood and frogs, wild beasts and pestilence, he is explicitly warned and disregards the warnings. Even when the plague causes him second thoughts, he sees its cessation as an opportunity to renege on his promises. And each time his stubbornness is expressed through the root h.z.k (strong) or the more intensive k.v.d (heavy). The different forms of the roots gradually show a King who begins simply obeying his natural tendency towards obstinacy, but eventually actively works at being stubborn, until finally, the new level of disobedience becomes his

new baseline, ingrained into his nature. When that process is complete, we no longer read that Pharaoh's heart hardens itself, nor that Pharaoh hardened his own heart; instead, the later plagues record that God hardened the heart of Pharaoh. Many commentators explain that by his earlier actions, Pharaoh enslaved himself to his wicked goal and ultimately deprived himself of the ability to choose.

When God redeemed the Israelites, He was inviting them to choose, and thereby to reverse for themselves the process that Pharaoh underwent. Once freed, the Israelites were to make themselves free, by accepting the law, by resolving never to do to others what was done to them, by caring for the defenseless, the disadvantaged, the stranger. Every day the test of how to express our freedom challenges us anew.

HIS MOST FAITHFUL SERVANT

Lord Voldemort's Death Eaters competed for the title.

Barty Crouch Jr. claimed it for his impersonation of Mad-Eye Moody in an attempt to deliver Harry to the Dark Lord. Bellatrix Lestrange, whose feelings towards Voldemort seemed to oscillate between worship and love, applied it to herself. Once

upon a time, even Lucius Malfoy saw himself in the running for the title "his most faithful servant." What would they have said if they knew that the phrase originated in the Bible?

When Miriam and Aaron spoke disparagingly about their brother Moses, God Himself defended his prophet. "My servant Moses is not such (i.e. not comparable to any other prophet)—of all my house he is the most faithful" (Numbers 12:7). And yet the usages could not be any more different.

What does it mean to be a faithful servant to Voldemort? If Lucius Malfoy is any indication, it means to attempt to ride the coattails of the Dark Lord to power and wealth based on racist and ruthless policies.

It also means that while you may admire, worship, and even love your boss, he views you only instrumentally, as a tool for advancing his goals. Should you fail him, do not expect a second chance. If your goals interfere with his, do not expect forbearance or a gentle refocusing.

And a servant of the Almighty? Rabbi Ezra Bick in his recent volume analyzing the *Amidah* prayer, explains why prayer is called *Avodah She'ba-lev*, service of the heart. It is the job of the servant to have no will other than that of his master. However, when that master is God, His will is that which is best for the servant. By serving his master, the servant of God is guaranteed to develop into the best person he or she can be.

The Dark Lord and his servants are locked in a cycle of selfishness, while the supreme King of Kings and his faithful are

engaged in mutual generosity and solicitude. The Biblical book that best reflects these contrasting types of relationships is the Book of Esther. King Ahasuerus and his courtiers, Haman prominent among them, live to exploit each other. By contrast, Esther and Mordechai seek to cooperate and present each other in the most flattering of ways.

FROM THE BREAD OF POVERTY TO GREAT WEALTH

We open the Seder by pointing to the Matzah and remembering that it represents the poverty we experienced in Egypt. But when we ate the same Matzah on our way out of servitude, it no longer represented poverty, but freedom. We recount how this reversal of fortune was foretold to our ancestor Abraham, when God told him of the impending slavery, but added that we would ultimately leave "with great wealth." Thus our deliverance is poised not only between slavery and freedom, but between poverty and wealth, as well.

The contrast between rich and poor is a recurring theme in the Harry Potter novels too. Without calling him poor, the first book makes it clear that Harry's lot at the Dursleys is one of penury. Dependent upon his stingy relatives for every scrap of food and every stitch of clothing, Harry is keenly aware of his impoverished state compared to that of Dudley.

The comparison of their birthday presents makes that even clearer, when Petunia labors to buy Dudley his 37th birthday present, while Harry's gift is Uncle Vernon's old socks. In this way, Harry's emergence from the Muggle world to the Wizarding world is both a movement from slavery to freedom and from poverty to the wealth his parents left him in Gringotts Bank.

Both the Jewish tradition and the Harry Potter novels encourage us to consider the proper uses of wealth and to examine what true wealth really is. Harry and Draco Malfoy are both wealthy, but relate to their wealth in totally different ways. To Draco, money confers status and grants the wealthy the right to feel superior to those less well heeled. His constant digs at Ron revolve around the Weasleys' modest means. He clearly inherited this attitude from his parents, who think nothing of buying Nimbus 2001 brooms for Draco's entire team to secure the position of Seeker for their son, and whose contributions to worthy causes elevate him above suspicion in the politically driven mind of Minister of Magic Cornelius Fudge. When Harry relates that Lucius Malfoy was one of the Death Eaters who joined the reborn Voldemort in the cemetery at the end of Book 4, Fudge replies, "Old wizarding family… contributions to all the right causes." Harry, on the other hand, sees his money as a tool for doing good. He gives his Triwizard tournament winnings to Fred and George Weasley as seed money for their joke shop. He buys Ron a pair of Omnioculars for the Quiddich World Cup. His generosity is reined in only by his desire not to embarrass those who might

EMPATHY FOR YOUR ENEMIES

As the ten plagues are recited, it is customary to pour drops of wine from one's cup. The most popular explanation for this custom is that when God's creatures are destroyed, even when their punishment is richly deserved, we cannot fully rejoice. The book of Proverbs warns, "When your enemy falls, do not be happy, and when he stumbles, let not your heart rejoice." How we would prefer to see the wicked repent and avert their punishment! The prophet Isaiah says of God, "For you have no desire for the death of the wicked; rather you wish to see him repent from his ways and live." According to the *midrash*, when the Egyptians drowned in the Red Sea, God stopped the angels from singing a hymn of praise: "My creatures are drowning in the Sea and you wish to sing?"

Such an attitude does not come naturally to most people. It must be modeled. God modeled empathy for one's enemy for the Jewish people. Dumbledore modeled it for Harry Potter. Throughout Book Six, Dumbledore is aware that Voldemort is trying to groom Dracoy Malfoy to murder the Headmaster. Instead of acting on the information to protect himself, Dumbledore enlists Snape to befriend Draco in order to save him from actually carrying out the mission. And on that fateful night

in the Astronomy Tower, when Draco disarms Dumbledore and is mere seconds from killing him, Dumbledore steers the conversation in the direction of giving Draco an honorable way out. He is more concerned with the state of Draco's soul than with his own survival. Harry is an apt student. On the night of the Battle of Hogwarts, Harry and Ron save Draco's life on several occasions, the most dramatic of which is an airborne rescue from the fiendfyre unleashed by Goyle in the Room of Requirement. But his true internalizing of the lesson of empathy is revealed in his final duel against Voldemort. Even as he feels the power and hatred building up in the Dark Lord's wand, and the Killing Curse seconds away, Harry finds the empathy to offer his arch enemy a way to escape his own accumulated evil. "Try for some remorse," he begs, to the disbelief of his implacable foe.

Student Voices – מתלמידי יותר מכולם

Who is the most generous character in Harry Potter?

★ Dumbledore – he shared his memories with Harry. *(Ilan G., grade 7)*

★ Snape – he gave his life for the cause. *(Benji R., grade 7)*

★ Sirius – he gave his house and his life for the cause.

★ Harry – he shared his invisibility cloak. *(Kayla S, grade 5)*

★ Ron – he never gets the credit but he's OK with it. *(Yahav R, grade 5)*

★ Hagrid – he helps Harry through all his challenges.

WHAT DO VILLAINS SEE IN THE MIRROR?

⚡

No bad guy will admit he's a bad guy. No villain wears a badge that says "I prey on innocent victims." In order to be able to look at himself in the mirror, a villain will adopt an inside-out view of the world, attributing noble motives to himself and nefarious intentions to his victims. He might even believe what he says.

Pharaoh did. As the worshipped head of a society built on slavery and domination, he had to justify enslaving the innocent descendants of Joseph, who had saved his country from famine just a generation earlier. And so he presented the project to his people as classic self-defense: "The nation of the children of Israel is more numerous and powerful than we are…when a war occurs, it will join our enemies and force us from the land." In other words, it isn't we who are enslaving the Hebrews—they have designs on our land and we are merely defending ourselves. What a deft reversal of victimizer and victim.

Rabbi Naftali Zvi Yehuda Berlin saw this in the words of the verse. *Vayare'u otanu ha-Mitzrim* is not the optimal way to say "The Egyptians acted evilly towards us." That would be "*Vayare'u Lanu.*" As it stands, the verse could just as easily be

translated "The Egyptians made us out to be the bad guys."

This is also the trademark behavior of Lord Voldemort and Rita Skeeter. Rita Skeeter's mantra is "The public has the right to know," casting herself as a crusader for truth, without bothering to mention that her brand of truth is more a combination of settling personal scores, creating scandal, and inventing lies as rapidly as her Quick-Quotes Quill can compose them. In her hands, people become caricatures of themselves. Shy, self-conscious Hermione becomes a femme-fatale; gentle Hagrid becomes a hulking menace, and, of course, Harry becomes whatever will sell more newspapers that particular day.

Voldemort was a master at exonerating—no, exalting himself, while recasting his victims as the real villains. His own criminality was excused by his philosophy that ""There is no good and evil, there is only power, and those too weak to seek it." Once he has established himself as having the courage to take his due, those who oppose him are simply too cowardly to join him. That alone would warrant their destruction, but Harry, in particular, is guilty of many other offenses. Like Dumbledore, Harry is misguided in his ascribing significance to the power of love. Moreover, his cowardice is amplified by his hiding behind others, like his parents, Sirius, and Dumbledore, to fight his battles. If left unharmed, Harry would prevent the realization of a new world order, in which Wizards would occupy their rightful place and Muggles and Mudbloods would recognize their

inferior status. For the sake of the Wizarding world, Harry must be destroyed. He, not Voldemort, is the threat.

SEEING OURSELVES THROUGH THE EYES OF OUR ENEMIES

Self-revelation can come from the strangest sources.

The Children of Israel arrived in Egypt as a family—*Ish u-ve-ito ba'u*. Numbering only 70 individuals, they saw themselves as, simply, the displaced descendants of Jacob, also known as Israel. With time their numbers grew, but their self-perception stayed the same. It was Pharaoh who first told us that we were not a family or a clan any longer, but a nation: "Behold, the nation of Bnei Yisrael is more numerous and powerful than we are." He gave us this title to implant in his Egyptian audience the sense of threat and menace.

Harry Potter hadn't given much thought to future career plans until Book Four. It is then that Mad-Eye Moody suggests that he would make a fine Auror, or hunter of dark wizards. The problem is—it wasn't really Moody who said that. It was Barty Crouch Jr., himself a Death Eater, who was impersonating Moody through the use of Polyjuice Potion. And yet the idea stuck with Harry, surfacing again in Book Five when

Harry is interviewed by Prof. McGonagall about his plans, and then challenged by Prof. Umbridge. How can you learn your innermost yearnings from your enemies?

It seems that you can. As the Rambam (Maimonides) is famous for saying, "Accept the truth from whoever says it." Perhaps our enemies, bent on understanding us in order to harm us, have a unique perspective on our strengths and weaknesses, less clouded by wishful thinking or false modesty. But that doesn't mean that we need to uncritically accept their view of us as accurate. They are certainly susceptible to biases and faulty assumptions. Pharaoh assumed that mere numbers and strength are enough to confer nation status. God, it seems, feels otherwise. When he charges us to be "a kingdom of priests and a holy nation," He adds the final ingredient to our nationhood: common mission and purpose as His ambassadors. Barty Crouch Jr. could not realize that his suggestion hit home precisely because Harry was committed to justice even at the expense of the ultimate self-sacrifice, not merely for the thrill of the chase or the stimulation of the puzzle.

Our enemies have the vision of determined hatred. It is our job to extract the kernel of accuracy and surround it with the cocoon of the values they lack.

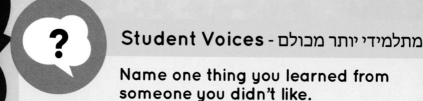

Student Voices - מתלמידי יותר מכולם

Name one thing you learned from someone you didn't like.

★ Sometimes you have to ignore people.
   (Honor G., grade 6)
★ Be yourself. *(Ariella B., grade 8)*
★ That pain causes you to make other people feel pain.
   (Hannah W., grade 6)
★ To see things from other people's perspective.
   (Tani L., Grade 8)
★ That even the worst people have some good inside of
   them. *(Jessica B., grade 8)*
★ To not give up. *(Emily F., grade 8)*
★ Not to judge people right away. *(Talia S., grade 5)*

The HEBREW section begins here.
Please open from the
opposite cover.

The ENGLISH section begins here.
Please open from the
opposite cover.

ACKNOWLEDGEMENTS

It's hard to believe that the first Harry Potter evening that I led was over fifteen years ago. The overwhelming response of my students inspired a journey that has culminated in this volume. Those students of the SAR Academy in Riverdale, New York have my deepest thanks. Their unflagging enthusiasm for all things Potter has rekindled my own time and time again. The administration of SAR, led first by Rabbi Joel Cohn, and then by Rabbi Binyamin Krauss, has always understood that education comes in many forms and that sometimes the most valuable experiences come at the expense of classroom hours, rather than during them. I am eternally grateful.

Congregation Etz Chaim of Kew Gardens Hills, where I have served for over two decades, is used to my idiosyncrasies. I am thankful daily for the good fortune of having spent much of life and raised my family in the midst of this unpretentious, welcoming, and understanding group of people.

It has been a great source of pride to watch my own children progress from being participants in those school events to being, in every real sense, my editors in my literary projects. They have fact-checked, encouraged, publicized, and shared my passion for both Harry Potter and Torah. Yair, in the meantime, has launched a remarkable journalistic career; Sarah Meira has become a writer, editor, and podcaster at large; they have truly edited this work, with SM setting up and taking charge of my Facebook page. Gavriel has been a great source of encouragement all the way through, Hudy has become a self-appointed publicity ambassador, even to the point of prowling the aisles of Yeshiva University's Seforim Sale and making sure that

customers see my books. Bracha and Duly have actually contributed illustrations that are being used to promote the Haggadah. Yisrael Dovid, who was a little young for my first book, has become a full partner in this endeavor, even correcting a quotation.

If my overblown Rabbinic English has successfully been reduced to readability, it is often thanks to the first journalist of the family, my brother Abe. The media trailblazer in our family is my brother Mordechai and his company ChadishMedia.

It must be maddening to be married to someone who is always coming up with "The Idea" of the century, despite not yet having properly developed the last great scheme. Putting up with me is only one of Dina Rosenberg's many talents. Being an inexhaustible source of giving, knowing what is truly important, and making life an adventure are a few more.

This project was merely words on a hard drive until I found Aviva Shur, who immediately shared my vision and translated it into elegant artistic form. She then expertly shepherded it through the publication process. Thanks to her, The Unofficial Hogwarts Haggadah is a reality.

I would like to acknowledge the generosity of Jewish Interactive, makers of JIStudio and other quality Jewish educational games, apps and programs, for their kind permission to use images from their library.

Finally, and perhaps most importantly, I owe a deep debt of gratitude to J.K. Rowling, whose deep understanding of the human condition, perfect sense of balance between the humorous and the serious, and knack for creating memorable characters, dialogue, settings, and just about everything, have enriched my life more than I can say.

THE
(unofficial)
HOGWARTS
HAGGADAH

MOSHE ROSENBERG

To Dina - my daily proof of a good God.
To the SAR Academy - so much more than a school
and
To Congregation Etz Chaim of Kew Gardens Hills - my spiritual home

Design by Aviva Shur.
Texts adapted from Wikipedia.
Translations partially adapted from OpenSiddur.org.

For the latest information on the Haggadah and to order more
copies, visit us on Facebook at
http://www.facebook.com/HPHaggadah.

The following images are attributed to Vecteezy.com:
Cover: glasses, bolt, wine glass
Page 6: broomstick, scroll
Page 7: Hogwarts castle, wand
Page 9: candle, feather
Page 10: loaf of bread
Page 14: leaf, table setting, book, musical notes
Page 15: parsley, book
Page 73: waves
Page 90: door

INTRODUCTION

A Hogwarts Haggadah? Are you kidding?

What could a School of Witchcraft and Wizardry possibly have in common with the most published book in Jewish history and the most celebrated holiday of the Jewish calendar?

As it turns out, quite a lot.

From the concepts of slavery and freedom, to the focus on education, to the number four, Harry Potter and Passover share almost everything. It's amazing that this book hasn't been written before.

I believe you can find valuable life lessons in the Torah and in Harry Potter. I hope after reading this Haggadah you'll have a deeper understanding of both. That was the goal I set when I wrote *Morality for Muggles: Ethics in the Bible and the World of Harry Potter* (KTAV, 2011). Since then I have found a term for it—Rav Aharon Lichtenstein, the late Rosh Yeshiva of Yeshivat Har Etzion, called such a process "reciprocal resonance." I take that to mean that each will create associations in our minds that will help us better appreciate the other.

I hope that, as a result of learning this Haggadah, Torah and Harry Potter resonate reciprocally in your hearts, and that you come away with the message that everything you read, learn, and experience can be drawn upon to deepen your service of God.

The Hogwarts Haggadah can be used both as an actual Haggadah at the Seder Table and as pleasant and thought-provoking reading over the entire year. It contains every word of the traditional text in both Hebrew and English. Alongside most pages are brief commentaries that are ideal for the night of the Seder. And together with those commentaries you'll find the voices of children who are, after all, the stars of the Seder. I asked my students and their friends to respond to questions related to each topic. I think you'll find their answers disarming, thought-provoking, and entertaining—and that the questions can serve as excellent conversation starters for your own Seder. Finally, after the conclusion of the Haggadah, I have included longer essays on particularly rich topics of discussion. These are not brief enough to snack on, but can provide rewarding reading and deeper insights.

I truly enjoyed writing The (Unofficial) Hogwarts Haggadah and hope you enjoy reading it!

זרוע
SHANKBONE

ביצה
EGG

חזרת
BITTER HERB

פסח

כרפס
KARPAS

חרוסת
HAROSET

מרור
MAROR

CHOREOGRAPHY OF A CASTLE...AND A FEAST

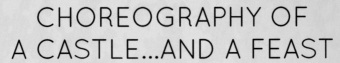

Notwithstanding an unpredictable staircase here and there, Hogwarts is a meticulously choreographed work of art. Every successive book reveals new secrets of the building and the grounds, all of which coalesce into a whole that simply couldn't have been otherwise. Even without amusement parks, Harry Potter fans live in this enchanted place.

Choreography is also vital to the Seder evening. The word *Seder* ("order") itself implies that every detail has its place without which the whole would be diminished. The concrete symbol of that order is the Seder plate, whose sturdy fixedness promises that each of its items will have its moment at precisely the right time. The mnemonic outline "*Kadesh…u'rehatz…,*" sung by many between each completed task and the next, is the verbal form of this choreography. But it doesn't end there: any host charged with seating the varied parade of guests who recline only once a year together is worthy of consideration for a Nobel Peace Prize.

BEDIKAT HAMETZ:
THE SEARCH FOR HAMETZ

On the evening before Passover, families gather to search for any remaining hametz in their already carefully cleaned homes. Traditionally, we use a candle for illumination, though a flashlight is also fine. We strategically plant ten small pieces of hametz around the home to be found. (Helpful tips: Use the kind that doesn't make crumbs, such as macaroni, and make sure the "planter" will remember where they are!) We make a blessing and the search begins… We burn the collected pieces (or otherwise dispose of them) in the morning.

We bless You, Hashem our God, Ruler of the Universe, Who has made us holy with His commandments, and commanded us about the removal of Hametz.

בָּרוּךְ אַתָּה יְהֹוָה אֱלֹהֵינוּ מֶלֶךְ
הָעוֹלָם אֲשֶׁר קִדְּשָׁנוּ בְּמִצְוֹתָיו
וְצִוָּנוּ עַל בִּיעוּר חָמֵץ:

All of the Harry Potter saga can be reduced to a search. At first Harry seeks a father figure and a way to deal with the deaths of his parents. Later, he thinks that what he is looking for is behind a door in the Ministry of Magic. But only in Book Seven does he actually get to choose for himself what to seek—will it be Horcruxes or Hallows? His answer leads

him to complete his own version of *Bedikat Hametz*, a search that tracks down each treacherous fragment of Voldemort's diseased soul and that ultimately compels him to look inside himself to see if he has absorbed some of that same disease. There is a time when Harry thinks that he must die to eradicate the evil of Voldemort that lingers within him. But it turns out that wizarding *hametz* can be found and eliminated and its vessels can purify themselves, not through the fire or boiling water we use to purge from *hametz*, but through self-sacrifice and the willingness to die for others. When Harry goes willingly into the Forbidden Forest to die in order to destroy the Horcrux Voldemort inadvertently made of him, he repeats the sacrifice of his mother and duplicates for his loved ones the protection that his mother had provided him.

BITTUL HAMETZ:
NULLIFYING THE HAMETZ

Not sufficing with searching out any last hametz, *we also verbally declare any remnants to be ownerless. This is done twice—once at night after the search, and again the next morning, right before the time that it becomes prohibited. The second declaration covers any* hametz *left for breakfast or for the purpose of burning. If the Aramaic text is daunting, the* bittul *may be recited in English.*

Any Hametz that is in my possession, which I did not see and remove, and which I do not know about, shall be as if it does not exist and shall become ownerless, like the dust of the earth.

כָּל חֲמִירָא וַחֲמִיעָא דְּאִיכָּא בִּרְשׁוּתִי דְּלָא חֲמִתֵּיה וּדְלָא בַעַרְתֵּיה וּדְלָא יְדַעְנָא לֵיה לִבָּטֵל וְלֶהֱוֵי הֶפְקֵר כְּעַפְרָא דְאַרְעָא:

GOBLINS AND
GLAZED DONUTS

It is debatable whether Griphook the goblin could have performed the ceremony of *Bittul Hametz*. You see, goblin concepts of ownership differ greatly from those in both the Muggle and Wizarding worlds, and certainly from that of Jewish law. Goblins are unable to relinquish ownership—they believe that even when they sell an object which they have made, like the sword of Godric Gryffindor or Aunt Muriel's tiara, it only leaves their hands temporarily, with ownership reverting back automatically after the purchaser's life. It would be amusing to investigate other legal systems to see if such unshakeable ownership would be problematic in disposing of *hametz*. One of the things that *Bittul Hametz* teaches us is the need to let go, and not to become too attached to our possessions, be they food, financial, or electronic. If they stand in the way of the fulfillment of a moral duty, our choice is clear. Sometimes it is instructive to see what we are like when our accustomed props are removed, our morning coffee delayed, or our smartphone on the fritz. (For a more extensive discussion of the different outlooks on ownership, see my *Morality for Muggles,* Chapter 3.)

BURNING THE HAMETZ

Although it is permissible to dispose of the last bits of hametz *in any manner, many choose to burn them during the morning of* Erev Pesach. *The second nullification declaration is recited.*

Any Hametz that is in my possession, whether I did or did not recognize it, whether I did or did not see it, whether I did or did not remove it, shall be as if it does not exist and shall become ownerless, like the dust of the earth.

כָּל חֲמִירָא וַחֲמִיעָא דְאִיכָּא בִּרְשׁוּתִי דַחֲזִתֵּיה וּדְלָא חֲזִתֵּיה דַחֲמִתֵּיה וּדְלָא חֲמִתֵּיה דְּבַעֲרְתֵּיה וּדְלָא בַעֲרְתֵּיה לִבָּטֵל וְלֶהֱוֵי הֶפְקֵר כְּעַפְרָא דְאַרְעָא:

THE HARDEST HAMETZ
TO FIND

During the weeks leading up to Pesach we scour our homes, our garments, our pantries to locate and destroy every last vestige of *hametz*. But that's only the preparation. Once we have rid ourselves of external leaven, we look within. We discover that *hametz* is a metaphor for every impulse that urges us to metaphorically puff ourselves up and take up more than our rightful place. The true search for and disposal of *hametz* is the character refinement that we perform in the Hebrew month of Nissan, where Passover falls. One lesser known opinion in the Talmud maintains that the beginning of Nisan is the correct Rosh Hashanah.

Dumbledore gave Harry just enough clues to seek out and destroy all but one of the horcruxes that tethered Voldemort to life. But there was one horcrux that Dumbledore kept secret. He only revealed it to Harry on the night of the battle of Hogwarts, through Snape's memory in the Pensieve. The final horcrux was Harry himself, and he had to be purged of it before Voldemort could be defeated once and for all. It was Harry's self-sacrifice that enabled the eradication of the final *hametz* of the Dark Lord and made ready the Seder to follow.

MAROR-מָרוֹר

 KOREKH-כּוֹרֵךְ

 SHULHAN OREKH
שֻׁלְחָן עוֹרֵךְ

 TZAFUN-צָפוּן

 BAREKH-בָּרֵךְ

 HALLEL-הַלֵּל

 NIRTZAH-נִרְצָה

KADESH - קַדֵּשׁ
RECITING KIDDUSH

U'REHATZ - וּרְחַץ

KARPAS - כַּרְפַּס

YAHATZ - יַחַץ
SPLITTING THE MIDDLE MATZAH

MAGGID - מַגִּיד
TELLING THE STORY

RAHTZAH - רָחְצָה

MOTZI-MATZAH - מוֹצִיא מַצָּה

KADESH - קַדֵּשׁ

RECITING KIDDUSH

Recite the following Kiddush over a full cup of wine or grape juice:

On Friday night begin:
And there was evening and there was morning, the sixth day. Now the heavens and all their host were completed. And on the seventh day God finished His work of creation which He had made. And God blessed the seventh day and made it holy, for on that day God rested from His work and ceased creating.

On all other days begin:
Blessed are You, Lord our God, Ruler of the universe, Who has chosen us from among all people, and languages, and made us holy through Your mitzvot, giving us lovingly [Shabbat for rest] festivals for joy, and special times for celebration, this [Shabbat and this] Passover, [given in love] this sacred gathering

בְּשַׁבָּת מַתְחִילִין

וַיְהִי עֶרֶב וַיְהִי בֹקֶר יוֹם הַשִּׁשִּׁי. וַיְכֻלּוּ הַשָּׁמַיִם וְהָאָרֶץ וְכָל צְבָאָם. וַיְכַל אֱלֹהִים בַּיּוֹם הַשְּׁבִיעִי מְלַאכְתּוֹ אֲשֶׁר עָשָׂה וַיִּשְׁבֹּת בַּיּוֹם הַשְּׁבִיעִי מִכָּל מְלַאכְתּוֹ אֲשֶׁר עָשָׂה. וַיְבָרֶךְ אֱלֹהִים אֶת יוֹם הַשְּׁבִיעִי וַיְקַדֵּשׁ אוֹתוֹ כִּי בוֹ שָׁבַת מִכָּל מְלַאכְתּוֹ אֲשֶׁר בָּרָא אֱלֹהִים לַעֲשׂוֹת.

בַּחוֹל מַתְחִילִין:

סַבְרִי מָרָנָן וְרַבָּנָן וְרַבּוֹתַי בָּרוּךְ אַתָּה יְיָ אֱלֹהֵינוּ מֶלֶךְ הָעוֹלָם בּוֹרֵא פְּרִי הַגָּפֶן. בָּרוּךְ אַתָּה יְיָ אֱלֹהֵינוּ מֶלֶךְ הָעוֹלָם, אֲשֶׁר בָּחַר בָּנוּ מִכָּל עָם וְרוֹמְמָנוּ מִכָּל לָשׁוֹן וְקִדְּשָׁנוּ בְּמִצְוֹתָיו. וַתִּתֶּן לָנוּ יְיָ אֱלֹהֵינוּ בְּאַהֲבָה (בְּשַׁבָּת: שַׁבָּתוֹת לִמְנוּחָה וּ)מוֹעֲדִים לְשִׂמְחָה, חַגִּים וּזְמַנִּים לְשָׂשׂוֹן, אֶת יוֹם

to commemorate the Exodus from Egypt. You have chosen us, and you have sanctified us from among all other peoples. And [Shabbat and] Your holy festivals you have [lovingly and willingly,] joyfully granted us. Blessed are You Lord, Who sanctifies [Shabbat], Israel and the festivals.

(הַשַּׁבָּת הַזֶּה וְאֶת יוֹם) חַג הַמַּצּוֹת הַזֶּה, זְמַן חֵרוּתֵנוּ (בְּאַהֲבָה), מִקְרָא קֹדֶשׁ, זֵכֶר לִיצִיאַת מִצְרָיִם. כִּי בָנוּ בָחַרְתָּ וְאוֹתָנוּ קִדַּשְׁתָּ מִכָּל הָעַמִּים, (וְשַׁבָּת) וּמוֹעֲדֵי קָדְשֶׁךָ (בְּאַהֲבָה וּבְרָצוֹן,) בְּשִׂמְחָה וּבְשָׂשׂוֹן הִנְחַלְתָּנוּ. בָּרוּךְ אַתָּה יְיָ, מְקַדֵּשׁ (הַשַּׁבָּת וְ) יִשְׂרָאֵל וְהַזְּמַנִּים.

On Saturday night include:
Blessed are You Lord our God Ruler of the universe who created the lights of fire.Blessed are You, Lord our God, Ruler of the universe, who makes a distinction between the holy and profane, light and darkness, Israel and the nations, Shabbat and the six workdays. You have made a distinction between the holiness of Shabbat and the holiness of the festival, and You have sanctified Shabbat above the six work-days. You have set apart and made holy Your people Israel with your holiness. Blessed are You, Lord, who distinguishes between degrees of sanctity.

בְּמוֹצָאֵי שַׁבָּת מוֹסִיפִין:
בָּרוּךְ אַתָּה יְיָ אֱלֹהֵינוּ מֶלֶךְ הָעוֹלָם, בּוֹרֵא מְאוֹרֵי הָאֵשׁ. בָּרוּךְ אַתָּה יְיָ אֱלֹהֵינוּ מֶלֶךְ הָעוֹלָם הַמַּבְדִּיל בֵּין קֹדֶשׁ לְחֹל, בֵּין אוֹר לְחֹשֶׁךְ, בֵּין יִשְׂרָאֵל לָעַמִּים, בֵּין יוֹם הַשְּׁבִיעִי לְשֵׁשֶׁת יְמֵי הַמַּעֲשֶׂה. בֵּין קְדֻשַּׁת שַׁבָּת לִקְדֻשַּׁת יוֹם טוֹב הִבְדַּלְתָּ, וְאֶת יוֹם הַשְּׁבִיעִי מִשֵּׁשֶׁת יְמֵי הַמַּעֲשֶׂה קִדַּשְׁתָּ. הִבְדַּלְתָּ וְקִדַּשְׁתָּ אֶת עַמְּךָ יִשְׂרָאֵל בִּקְדֻשָּׁתֶךָ. בָּרוּךְ אַתָּה יְיָ הַמַּבְדִּיל בֵּין קֹדֶשׁ לְקֹדֶשׁ.

Blessed are You, Lord our God, Ruler of the universe, who has sustained us, maintained us and enabled us to reach this moment.

בָּרוּךְ אַתָּה יְיָ אֱלֹהֵינוּ מֶלֶךְ הָעוֹלָם, שֶׁהֶחֱיָנוּ וְקִיְּמָנוּ וְהִגִּיעָנוּ לַזְּמַן הַזֶּה.

RAISE YOUR GLASS:
FOUR CUPS, FOUR TOASTS

Raising one's glass in a toast is a practice that spans cultures and centuries. The Greeks had it, as did the Romans. Sometimes the observance of toasting rituals was a pretext for excessive drinking. As in so many areas, Judaism elevated the custom by finding a way to make it a spiritual practice, which demonstrates celebration and gratitude without descending into base behavior. Rabbi Joseph H. Lookstein once explained, "Other cultures drink; the Jew says L'Chaim (to life)!" Jewish law adds solemnity and importance to many blessings, by pronouncing them over a cup of wine, which is then called *Kos shel Berakha* (cup of blessing). On the Seder night, there is an added facet to each of the four cups of wine; beyond the blessing which they enhance, they are also the concrete expressions of freedom, or *herut*. We toast God, the liberator. And at specific moments in the Haggadah's recitation, we simply lift our glass to God, in a sign of respect and thanksgiving.

This last form of toast echoes the unforgettable scene at the end of The Goblet of Fire, when Dumbledore, as a token of respect for their heroism and sacrifice, raises his goblet, first to Cedric Diggory, and then to Harry. There is no hint of drinking here; Professor Trelawney and Winky the house elf are the series's cautionary tales for the dangers of alcohol. The toast, in both Hogwarts and Halakha, is about honor and tribute to those who deserve them.

U'REHATZ- וּרְחַץ

Seder participants wash their hands in the manner usually done before eating bread, but do not recite the al netilat yadayim *blessing.*

VERBAL OR NONVERBAL

It is tempting to compare the act of washing without reciting the customary blessing to casting spells without verbal incantation, but the two are, in fact, diametrically opposed. While the ability to perform non-verbal magic demonstrates a more advanced grasp of the art and a more powerful wizardry, the absence of a blessing at this point in the Seder shows that

the obligation is actually a lesser one, an echo of an earlier age when ritual law required washing before eating anything that had been dipped in certain liquids.

KARPAS- כַּרְפַּס

A small amount of a vegetable (type varies by custom) dipped in salt water is distributed to each member of the Seder. The blessing of Boreh Peri Ha–adama *is recited and it is eaten. The Talmud explains that the unusual course is meant to pique the curiosity of children and elicit questions.*

Blessed are You, Lord, our God, Ruler of the universe, who creates the fruit of the earth.

בָּרוּךְ אַתָּה יְיָ אֱלֹהֵינוּ מֶלֶךְ הָעוֹלָם, בּוֹרֵא פְּרִי הָאֲדָמָה.

YAHATZ- יַחַץ
SPLITTING THE MIDDLE MATZAH

Half is put aside to be used later for Afikoman. *Kids know what to do about that.*

MAGGID- מַגִּיד

TELLING THE STORY

The leader of the Seder uncovers and points to the matzah.

This is the bread of affliction, which our ancestors ate in the land of Egypt. Let all who are hungry come and eat. Let all who are in need, come and share the Pesach meal. This year, we are here. Next year, in the land of Israel. This year, we are slaves. Next year, we will be free.

הָא לַחְמָא עַנְיָא דִי אֲכָלוּ אַבְהָתָנָא בְּאַרְעָא דְמִצְרָיִם. כָּל דִכְפִין יֵיתֵי וְיֵיכֹל, כָּל דִצְרִיךְ יֵיתֵי וְיִפְסַח. הָשַׁתָּא הָכָא, לְשָׁנָה הַבָּאָה בְּאַרְעָא דְיִשְׂרָאֵל. הָשַׁתָּא עַבְדֵי, לְשָׁנָה הַבָּאָה בְּנֵי חוֹרִין.

THE BREAD OF POVERTY

As the matzah can attest, one measure of wealth or poverty has always been culinary. The diet of the rich has always set itself apart from that of the poor. Once upon a time that meant that the rich were able to literally live off the "fat of the land," when fat was considered a sign of health and wealth. Now, it is often the more nutritious food choices that tend to be more expensive and are the domain of the well-to-do,

while the lower class subsists on cheaper, coarser, less healthy fare.

One of the very first scenes of Harry in the magical world reflects this reality. Harry, though a newcomer, has ample funds from his parents' vault at Gringotts to buy anything he wants from the candy trolley, and takes full advantage of his privileged status. Ron, on the other hand, takes out a dry sandwich from home, which, to him, represents the bread of poverty. To Harry's credit, he finds a way to share his good fortune with his friend. One of the lessons of the exodus is to use the memory of our own affliction to spare others the same travail.

The second cup is filled. Traditionally, the youngest person at the table asks the Four Questions.

Why is this night of Passover different from all other nights of the year?

מַה נִּשְׁתַּנָה הַלַּיְלָה הַזֶּה מִכָּל הַלֵּילוֹת?

On all other nights, we eat either leavened or unleavened bread, why on this night do we eat only matzah?

שֶׁבְּכָל הַלֵּילוֹת אָנוּ אוֹכְלִין חָמֵץ וּמַצָּה, הַלַּיְלָה הַזֶּה - כֻּלוֹ מַצָּה!?

On all other nights, we eat vegetables of all kinds, why on this night must we eat bitter herbs?

שֶׁבְּכָל הַלֵּילוֹת אָנוּ אוֹכְלִין שְׁאָר יְרָקוֹת, הַלַּיְלָה הַזֶּה מָרוֹר!?

On all other nights, we do not dip vegetables even once, why on this night do we dip greens into salt water and bitter herbs into haroset?

On all other nights, everyone sits up straight or reclines, why on this night do we all recline

שֶׁבְּכָל הַלֵּילוֹת אֵין אָנוּ מַטְבִּילִין אֲפִילוּ פַּעַם אֶחָת, הַלַּיְלָה הַזֶּה שְׁתֵּי פְעָמִים!?

שֶׁבְּכָל הַלֵּילוֹת אָנוּ אוֹכְלִין בֵּין יוֹשְׁבִין וּבֵין מְסֻבִּין, הַלַּיְלָה הַזֶּה כֻּלָּנוּ מְסֻבִּין!?

Student Voices - מתלמידי יותר מכולם

What Is A Question To Which You Have Never Received A Satisfactory Answer?

★ **What would God gain out of creating man?**
   (Gavi W., grade 7)
★ **How was Hashem created?** *(Rachel M., grade 6)*
★ **Why do bad things happen to good people?**
★ **Why can't I get a dog?** *(Julia D., grade 8)*
★ **Why does everyone have to grow up?**
   (Zahava K., grade 8)
★ **Why is "fridge" spelled with a "d," but "refrigerator" is not?** *(Merav S., grade 8)*
★ **Why does school matter when you have Google?**
   (Tamar P., grade 5)

Q&A

The question and answer format is no accident. The Torah commands: "When your child asks you...tell him/her..." Elsewhere children are commanded: "Ask your father and he will tell you." Parents are obligated to engage with their children on this evening, and are even given a script to get the ball rolling. Unusual table etiquette is meant to elicit questions (like the *karpas*). Should the child not rise to the occasion, the parent must take the initiative. Anyone who has tried to run a discussion at a Shabbat table knows the innate difficulties. Even so, on this special night, parents are told to pull out all the stops.

The best professors at Hogwarts were the ones who invited questions, like Remus Lupin or Albus Dumbledore. Snape, out of impatience, Umbridge, out of superiority (or was it insecurity), and Trelawney, out of incompetence, evaded questions. Their inaccessibility not only made it harder for students to learn, but made it almost impossible to develop a relationship. Judaism recognizes the meeting ground of sincere questioner and unintimidated respondent as fertile soil for forging a relationship between generations.

Uncover the matzot.

We were slaves to Pharaoh in Egypt, and the Lord, our God, took us out from there with a strong hand and with an outstretched arm. If the Holy One, blessed be He, had not taken our fathers out of Egypt, then we, our children and our children's children would have remained enslaved to Pharaoh in Egypt. Even if all of us were wise, all of us understanding, all of us knew the Torah, we would still be obligated to retell the exodus from Egypt; and everyone who discusses the exodus from Egypt at length is praiseworthy.

עֲבָדִים הָיִינוּ לְפַרְעֹה בְּמִצְרָיִם, וַיּוֹצִיאֵנוּ יְיָ אֱלֹהֵינוּ מִשָּׁם בְּיָד חֲזָקָה וּבִזְרוֹעַ נְטוּיָה. וְאִלּוּ לֹא הוֹצִיא הַקָּדוֹשׁ בָּרוּךְ הוּא אֶת אֲבוֹתֵינוּ מִמִּצְרַיִם, הֲרֵי אָנוּ וּבָנֵינוּ וּבְנֵי בָנֵינוּ מְשֻׁעְבָּדִים הָיִינוּ לְפַרְעֹה בְּמִצְרָיִם. וַאֲפִילוּ כֻּלָּנוּ חֲכָמִים, כֻּלָּנוּ נְבוֹנִים, כֻּלָּנוּ זְקֵנִים, כֻּלָּנוּ יוֹדְעִים אֶת הַתּוֹרָה, מִצְוָה עָלֵינוּ לְסַפֵּר בִּיצִיאַת מִצְרָיִם. וְכָל הַמַּרְבֶּה לְסַפֵּר בִּיצִיאַת מִצְרַיִם הֲרֵי זֶה מְשֻׁבָּח.

FROM NEGATIVE TO POSITIVE-מגנות לשבח
A COMPARISON OF STATES

"There is no happiness or sadness—only a comparison of states"
-Edmond Dantes, *The Count of Monte Cristo* by Alexandre Dumas

Success is counted sweetest
By those who ne'er succeed.
To comprehend a nectar
Requires sorest need.
-Emily Dickinson

The retelling of the story of the Exodus has specific rules. There is a prescribed time—the evening of the 15th of Nissan; a specific format—question and answer; a particular literary genre—midrashic exposition of Biblical verses; designated props—matzah and maror. And according to the Talmud, there is a required narrative trajectory—"One opens with the negative (*genut*) and concludes with the positive (*shevah*)." The quotations above may explain one reason for this order. To truly understand what God has done for us, we must relive where we were before He intervened. Gratitude isn't fully sincere if it comes from a place of total com-

fort. We must be slaves again to re-experience true freedom.

The love that Harry bears for Hogwarts and the Wizarding world is intensified by the fact that he begins each book living with the Dursleys and experiences his own annual exodus from oppression to appreciation. In effect, each novel begins with *genut* and builds to *shevah*.

Student Voices - מתלמידי יותר מכולם

Which Harry Potter character best understood the concept of freedom and why?

★ Dobby because he was a house elf and became a free elf.

★ Fred and George because they pursued their dreams and founded their store. *(Tiferet G., grade 8)*

★ Dumbledore because he let Harry make choices *(Talia P., grade 7)*

★ Hermione because she founded S.P.E.W. *(Benjy R., grade 7)*

★ Harry because he freed Dobby.

★ Ginny because she knew what it was like to be controlled. *(Gila S., grade 5)*

★ Luna because she lived her life her way. *(Tamar P., grade 5)*

It once happened that Rabbis Eliezer, Joshua, Elazar ben Azaryah, Akiva and Tarfon were reclining at the seder table in Bnei Brak. They spent the whole night discussing the Exodus until their students came and said to them: "Rabbis, it is time for us to recite the morning Shema."

Rabbi Elazar ben Azaryah said: "Although I am like a seventy-year old man, I had not succeeded in proving that the Exodus from Egypt should be mentioned at night, until Ben Zoma proved it by quoting: "In order that you may remember the day you left Egypt all the days of your life." The Torah adds the word "all" to the phrase "the days of your life" to indicate that the nights are meant as well. The sages declare that "the days of your life" means the present world and "all" includes the Messianic era.

מַעֲשֶׂה בְּרַבִּי אֱלִיעֶזֶר וְרַבִּי יְהוֹשֻׁעַ וְרַבִּי אֶלְעָזָר בֶּן עֲזַרְיָה וְרַבִּי עֲקִיבָא וְרַבִּי טַרְפוֹן שֶׁהָיוּ מְסֻבִּין בִּבְנֵי בְרַק, וְהָיוּ מְסַפְּרִים בִּיצִיאַת מִצְרַיִם כָּל אוֹתוֹ הַלַּיְלָה עַד שֶׁבָּאוּ תַלְמִידֵיהֶם וְאָמְרוּ לָהֶם: רַבּוֹתֵינוּ, הִגִּיעַ זְמַן קְרִיאַת שְׁמַע שֶׁל שַׁחֲרִית.

אָמַר רַבִּי אֶלְעָזָר בֶּן עֲזַרְיָה: הֲרֵי אֲנִי כְּבֶן שִׁבְעִים שָׁנָה, וְלֹא זָכִיתִי שֶׁתֵּאָמֵר יְצִיאַת מִצְרַיִם בַּלֵּילוֹת עַד שֶׁדְּרָשָׁהּ בֶּן זוֹמָא: שֶׁנֶּאֱמַר, לְמַעַן תִּזְכֹּר אֶת יוֹם צֵאתְךָ מֵאֶרֶץ מִצְרַיִם כֹּל יְמֵי חַיֶּיךָ, יְמֵי חַיֶּיךָ - הַיָּמִים, כָּל יְמֵי חַיֶּיךָ - הַלֵּילוֹת. וַחֲכָמִים אוֹמְרִים: יְמֵי חַיֶּיךָ - הָעוֹלָם הַזֶּה, כֹּל יְמֵי חַיֶּיךָ - לְהָבִיא לִימוֹת הַמָּשִׁיחַ.

Blessed is the Omnipresent One, blessed be He! Blessed is He who gave the Torah to His people Israel, blessed be He! The Torah speaks of four types of children: one is wise, one is wicked, one is simple, and one does not know how to ask.

The Wise One asks: "What is the meaning of the laws and traditions God has commanded?" You should teach him all the traditions of Passover,(up to and including the law that) we do not eat further dessert after the Paschal sacrifice.

The Wicked One asks: "What does this ritual mean to you?" By using the expression "to you" he excludes himself from his people and denies God. Blunt his teeth and say to him: "It is for the sake of this that the Lord did (miracles) for me when I came out of Egypt." "For me" and not for him, for had he been in Egypt, he would not have been redeemed.

בָּרוּךְ הַמָּקוֹם, בָּרוּךְ הוּא. בָּרוּךְ שֶׁנָּתַן תּוֹרָה לְעַמּוֹ יִשְׂרָאֵל, בָּרוּךְ הוּא. כְּנֶגֶד אַרְבָּעָה בָנִים דִּבְּרָה תּוֹרָה. אֶחָד חָכָם, וְאֶחָד רָשָׁע, וְאֶחָד תָּם, וְאֶחָד שֶׁאֵינוֹ יוֹדֵעַ לִשְׁאוֹל.

חָכָם מָה הוּא אוֹמֵר?
מָה הָעֵדוֹת וְהַחֻקִּים וְהַמִּשְׁפָּטִים אֲשֶׁר צִוָּה יְיָ אֱלֹהֵינוּ אֶתְכֶם? וְאַף אַתָּה אֱמָר לוֹ כְּהִלְכוֹת הַפֶּסַח: אֵין מַפְטִירִין אַחַר הַפֶּסַח אֲפִיקוֹמָן.

רָשָׁע מָה הוּא אוֹמֵר?
מָה הָעֲבֹדָה הַזֹּאת לָכֶם? לָכֶם - וְלֹא לוֹ. וּלְפִי שֶׁהוֹצִיא אֶת עַצְמוֹ מִן הַכְּלָל כָּפַר בְּעִקָּר. וְאַף אַתָּה הַקְהֵה אֶת שִׁנָּיו וֶאֱמָר לוֹ: בַּעֲבוּר זֶה עָשָׂה יְיָ לִי בְּצֵאתִי מִמִּצְרָיִם. לִי - וְלֹא לוֹ. אִילוּ הָיָה שָׁם, לֹא הָיָה נִגְאָל.

The Simple One asks: "What is all this?" You should tell him: "It was with a mighty hand that the Lord took us out of Egypt, out of the house of bondage."

As for the One Who Does Not Know How To Ask, you should open the discussion for him, as it is written: "And you shall tell your child on that day, It is for the sake of *this* that the Lord did (miracles) for me when I came out of Egypt."

תָּם מָה הוּא אוֹמֵר?
מַה זֹּאת? וְאָמַרְתָּ אֵלָיו:
בְּחֹזֶק יָד הוֹצִיאָנוּ יְיָ מִמִּצְרַיִם,
מִבֵּית עֲבָדִים.

וְשֶׁאֵינוֹ יוֹדֵעַ לִשְׁאוֹל -
אַתְּ פְּתַח לוֹ, שֶׁנֶּאֱמַר: וְהִגַּדְתָּ
לְבִנְךָ בַּיּוֹם הַהוּא לֵאמֹר,
בַּעֲבוּר זֶה עָשָׂה יְיָ לִי בְּצֵאתִי
מִמִּצְרָיִם.

Student Voices - מתלמידי יותר מכולם

Who are the smartest characters in Harry Potter and why?

★ Nicholas Flamel. *(Avner, grade 8)*
★ Snape because he knew that in order to help Harry, he had to be mean to him. *(Julia D., grade 8)*
★ Hedwig – She had a great sense of direction! *(Honor G., grade 5)*

ON THE VARIETIES
OF WISDOM

⚡

"Me!" said Hermione. "Books! And cleverness! There are more important things—friendship and bravery..." *(Harry Potter and the Sorcerer's Stone*, 1998).

Hermione reminds us that there are many ways to be a *Chacham*. Scholarship and book learning are only one. The different forms of wisdom in which Harry, Ron, and Hermione excelled were all tested by the protections placed around the Sorcerer's Stone. Sociologist Howard Gardner has famously catalogued seven forms of *Chochma* in which different people excel, calling them "multiple intelligences." Hermione's category of friendship would be what Gardner calls interpersonal intelligence.

Pirkei Avot recognizes that *Chochma* covers more than intellectual prowess, when it lists the seven attributes of a *Chacham*, which are really more examples of protocol and refined behavior, such as not speaking before someone who is greater in wisdom. Likewise, in explaining the "wisdom" of the daughters of Tzelophchad, who petitioned for a share in the land of Israel, some Midrashic views credit them with knowledge of the law, while others point to their impeccable timing. Wisdom comes in many varieties.

EDUCATION:
ONE SIZE DOES NOT FIT ALL

⚡

The most striking parallel between Hogwarts and Haggadah has to be the four houses of Hogwarts and the four children of the Seder. While they are not and need not be exactly correlated, these categories of students agree on a major principle of education—each student is an individual, endowed with unique character traits, aptitudes, and passions. While it is valuable for students with one bent to be exposed to those of differing strengths and natures, it is also necessary to have the opportunity to develop their own style, surrounded by those who share it. Gryffindors may take Potions with the Slytherins but they do not share the same common room with each other. And even within a house of Hogwarts or a genre of Seder child, shades of differences abound. It took a professor like Remus Lupin to realize that Harry Potter needed to be taught the Patronus charm years before his classmates, and only a teacher like Mad-Eye Moody (a counterfeit one at that) understood that the way to Neville's potential lay through Herbology and a mimbulus mimbletonia. Not every chacham is the Vilna Gaon of tomorrow. Some are focused on the mastery of Jewish Law, others are drawn to Bible studies and philosophy, and even others may become the Jewish historians of tomorrow. Part

of the thrill of constantly evolving educational technology is the ability to constantly measure individual progress and chart a highly individualized course of study at the perfect pace for each student. Surely that is what King Solomon meant when he wrote: "Educate each child according to his path."

 **Student Voices** - מתלמידי יותר מכולם

What is your favorite way to learn?

★ One-on-One ★ Projects ★ Songs ★ Games
★ Small Groups ★ Hands-on Activities ★ Debates
★ Stories ★ Chavruta (partners) ★ From a teacher
★ With an iPad ★ Acting Things Out
★ From Someone Passionate ★ Through Videos
★ Visually ★ By Myself ★ With Kahoot!
★ With a little bit of noise ★ By Magic
★ Sitting Down.

DESTROYING OR DEFANGING THE WICKED?

⚡

"If we die for them, Harry, I'll kill you!" *(Harry Potter and the Deathly Hallows, 2007)*

Ron could not understand why Harry, after rescuing the diadem of Ravenclaw and escaping the trap set by Malfoy, Crabbe, and Goyle, would risk his life to go back and rescue Draco from the fiendfyre let loose by Crabbe in the Room of Requirement. But Harry, like Dumbledore the year before, saw more than a Death Eater-in-Training in Draco Malfoy. He believed that there was good in Malfoy that was worth saving, if only one could get past the threatening exterior.

The same attitude characterizes the treatment of the Wicked Son by some commentators on the Haggadah. One such approach is cited by Rabbi Jonathan Sacks, who notes that the numerical value of Rasha (wicked) is 570, while the value of Tzaddik (righteous) is 204. To turn a Rasha into a Tzaddik, you must merely subtract his fangs (*"hakeh es shinav"* – "blunt his teeth") because the value of "shinav"/"his teeth" is 366. Take away the threatening but superficial fangs of the Wicked Son (570 - 366) and you will see his true righteous potential beneath them (204).

One might think that the Haggadah can be recited on the first day of the month of Nisan. Therefore the Torah says: "You shall tell your son on that day" [the first day of Passover]. One might think that the phrase "on that day" means that the story of the Exodus may be recited in the daytime; therefore, the Torah says: "It was for the sake of *this* that the Lord did for me." The word *this* refers to the time when the matzo and the maror are placed before you - on Passover night when you are obliged to eat them.

At first our forefathers worshiped idols, but now the Omnipresent has brought us near to Divine service, as it is written: "Joshua said to all the people: So says the Lord God of Israel-your fathers had always lived beyond the Euphrates River, Terah the father of Abraham and Nahor; they worshipped other gods. I took your father Abraham from

יָכוֹל מֵרֹאשׁ חֹדֶשׁ, תַּלְמוּד לוֹמַר בַּיּוֹם הַהוּא, אִי בַּיּוֹם הַהוּא יָכוֹל מִבְּעוֹד יוֹם, תַּלְמוּד לוֹמַר בַּעֲבוּר זֶה - בַּעֲבוּר זֶה לֹא אָמַרְתִּי אֶלָּא בְּשָׁעָה שֶׁיֵּשׁ מַצָּה וּמָרוֹר מֻנָּחִים לְפָנֶיךָ.

מִתְּחִלָּה עוֹבְדֵי עֲבוֹדָה זָרָה הָיוּ אֲבוֹתֵינוּ, וְעַכְשָׁיו קֵרְבָנוּ הַמָּקוֹם לַעֲבֹדָתוֹ, שֶׁנֶּאֱמַר: וַיֹּאמֶר יְהוֹשֻׁעַ אֶל כָּל הָעָם, כֹּה אָמַר יְיָ אֱלֹהֵי יִשְׂרָאֵל: בְּעֵבֶר הַנָּהָר יָשְׁבוּ אֲבוֹתֵיכֶם מֵעוֹלָם, תֶּרַח אֲבִי אַבְרָהָם וַאֲבִי נָחוֹר, וַיַּעַבְדוּ אֱלֹהִים אֲחֵרִים. וָאֶקַּח אֶת אֲבִיכֶם אֶת אַבְרָהָם מֵעֵבֶר הַנָּהָר וָאוֹלֵךְ אוֹתוֹ בְּכָל אֶרֶץ כְּנַעַן, וָאַרְבֶּה אֶת זַרְעוֹ וָאֶתֶּן לוֹ אֶת יִצְחָק, וָאֶתֵּן לְיִצְחָק אֶת יַעֲקֹב וְאֶת עֵשָׂו. וָאֶתֵּן לְעֵשָׂו אֶת הַר שֵׂעִיר לָרֶשֶׁת אֹתוֹ, וְיַעֲקֹב וּבָנָיו יָרְדוּ מִצְרָיִם.

the other side of the river and led him through all the land of Canaan. I multiplied his family and gave him Isaac. To Isaac I gave Jacob and Esau; to Esau I gave Mount Seir to inherit. However Jacob and his children went down to Egypt."

YAAKOV U'VANAV YARDU
PAYING THE PRICE

The most precious things in life are only obtained by those willing to pay the price. The Talmud (*Berakhot 5a*) says that three precious gifts were granted the Jewish people—Torah, the World to Come, and the land of Israel—and all three can only be acquired through undergoing affliction. The Haggadah records that God gave Esau the land of Seir with no strings attached. Jacob and his family, however, had to go down to Egypt and be tempered in the crucible of slavery to earn the gift of the land of Israel.

As early as Book One, Harry is aware that fighting the good fight can carry a steep price, but he is willing to pay it. When he thinks that his friends are trying to dissuade him from going after the Sorcerer's Stone, he declares, "Losing points doesn't matter any more, can't you see? … If I get caught before I can get to the stone, well, I'll have to go back to the Dursleys and wait for Voldemort to find me there, it's only dying a little bit later than I would have, because I'm never going over to the Dark Side!"

Student Voices - מתלמידי יותר מכולם

What is something worth sacrificing for?

★ Family, Friends, My dog...
★ Hashem. *(Sam M., grade 8)*
★ Giving up hobbies to do better in school.
  (Kiki L., grade 7)
★ I would sacrifice my phone for family.
  (Talia A., grade 7)
★ I would give up social media not to be a diabetic.
  (Deva L., grade 7)
★ Cinnamon Buns. *(Nate G., grade 5)*

Blessed be He who keeps His promise to Israel; blessed be He. The Holy One, blessed be He, calculated the time for our final deliverance in order to fulfill what He had pledged to our father Abraham inin the "Covenant between the pieces", as it is written: "He said to Abram, 'Know that your descendants will sojourn in a land that is not their own, and (the host nation) will enslave and afflict them for four hundred years; however, I will punish the nation that enslaved them, and afterward they shall leave with great wealth."

בָּרוּךְ שׁוֹמֵר הַבְטָחָתוֹ לְיִשְׂרָאֵל, בָּרוּךְ הוּא. שֶׁהַקָּדוֹשׁ בָּרוּךְ הוּא חִשַּׁב אֶת הַקֵּץ, לַעֲשׂוֹת כְּמַה שֶׁאָמַר לְאַבְרָהָם אָבִינוּ בִּבְרִית בֵּין הַבְּתָרִים, שֶׁנֶּאֱמַר: וַיֹּאמֶר לְאַבְרָם, יָדֹעַ תֵּדַע כִּי גֵר יִהְיֶה זַרְעֲךָ בְּאֶרֶץ לֹא לָהֶם, וַעֲבָדוּם וְעִנּוּ אֹתָם אַרְבַּע מֵאוֹת שָׁנָה. וְגַם אֶת הַגּוֹי אֲשֶׁר יַעֲבֹדוּ דָּן אָנֹכִי וְאַחֲרֵי כֵן יֵצְאוּ בִּרְכֻשׁ גָּדוֹל.

CHISHAV ET HA-KETZ

Timing is everything. The "*ketz*," or end is the term given
to represent the moment of redemption. It could not be too
early. The prophecy given Abraham foretelling 400 years
had to be satisfied somehow. The Midrash tells of some children of tribe of Ephraim who attempted to leave earlier and
were massacred. Yet it could not be too late or there would
be no identifiable Jewish people to redeem. The Rabbis say
that the Children of Israel had descended to the 49th gate of
impurity and that from the 50th there is no return. And so
God needed to "calculate the *ketz*" to come about at precisely the right moment. One calculation has the Children of
Israel leaving after 210 years, with 190 being "forgiven" due
to the intensity of the enslavement. Fortuitously, "*ketz*," in
numerical terms equals 190.

Harry's quest was also tightly tethered to timing. Most of the
way, it is a race against time to find and destroy every Horcrux before the final showdown. When things go too slow-
ly, there is frustration and dissension in the ranks. Yet there
was also an element of having to avoid the urge to hastily
switch focus and pursue Hallows, rather than Horcuxes. It is
there that Dumbledore finally confesses, "I counted on Miss
Granger to slow you down." The *ketz* arrives when Harry
and Hogwarts are ready, but barely.

BRIT BEIN HA-BETARIM:
SLAVERY FORETOLD
PROPHECY AND CHOICE

While the Jewish and Wizarding worlds both have a tradition of prophecy, they differ in many crucial aspects. The character of the prophet, the source of prophecy and the means of preserving prophetic messages differ radically. Sybil Trelawney is no Jeremiah, God doesn't figure into the magical message, and the Jewish Temple contained no hall of prophecy. Yet in one key question the two traditions agree: Prophecy does not preclude free will.

At the end of Book Five, when he finally reveals to Harry the existence of the prophecy that Voldemort sought, Dumbledore makes clear to Harry that he need not fight Voldemort simply because the prophecy declared that "Neither can live while the other survives." Harry still had a choice and, to him, that made all the difference. The very same point is made by Biblical commentators who ask why Pharaoh deserved to be punished if his enslavement of the Hebrews was foretold to Abraham. The Rambam (Maimonides) replies that Pharaoh was not bound to fulfill the prophecy, God could see to its fulfillment on one way or another. Pharaoh had total freedom in choosing his path.

Cover the matzot. Everyone should raise their cup and recite:

It was this covenant which stood by our ancestors and us. For it was not one (foe) alone who rose up against us to destroy us. Rather, in every generation there are those who rise up to destroy us, but the Holy One blessed be He saves us from their hands.

וְהִיא שֶׁעָמְדָה לַאֲבוֹתֵינוּ וְלָנוּ! שֶׁלֹּא אֶחָד בִּלְבָד עָמַד עָלֵינוּ לְכַלּוֹתֵנוּ, אֶלָּא שֶׁבְּכָל דּוֹר וָדוֹר עוֹמְדִים עָלֵינוּ לְכַלּוֹתֵנוּ, וְהַקָּדוֹשׁ בָּרוּךְ הוּא מַצִּילֵנוּ מִיָּדָם.

B'KHOL DOR VADOR:
THE CYCLICAL NATURE OF THE STRUGGLE

American Jews in the year 2017 can identify with this passage. Some of us, having grown up in an America that had become more and more tolerant of differences, dared to hope that anti-Semitism was a scourge of the past which would be finally consigned to the dustbin of history. Sadly, rising anti-Semitic acts in the U.S. have shattered that hope and left us feeling that our enlightened generation was the exception, rather than the rule. It is now time to fight the

recurring cancer once more. Can it ever be defeated for good? We can only do our part and hope for the fulfillment of the words of the prophets who foresaw a final victory of good over evil.

The arc of the Harry Potter novels confirms this cyclical vision of the battle against evil. Lord Voldemort was unexpectedly stymied ten years before the series begins, and is hoped dead by the majority of the wizarding world, from Minister of Magic Cornelius Fudge on down. But those truly wise understood from the start that there would be a return and planned for it. Evil would rise from the ashes and so must good—hence, the Order of the Phoenix. Will there be a final victory for good? Dumbledore let Harry hope for just that, when helping him decide whether to return from "Kings Cross Station." It appears that evil was defeated with finality in the Battle of Hogwarts. Or was it...

Student Voices - מתלמידי יותר מכולם

What was the most difficult choice you have ever had to make?

★ What school to go to.
★ Whether to do something my friends were doing.
★ To become a vegetarian. *(Moshe S., grade 5)*
★ Whether to be friends with someone. *(Mia F., grade 8)*
★ Israel or Universal Studios. *(Alex W., grade 5)*

How do you know if you can trust someone?

★ If they keep a secret. *(Zahava K., grade 8)*
★ If they stand by me through good and bad.
  (Deva L., grade 7)
★ You don't – you have to take a chance. *(Ella W., grade 6)*
★ If you pinky promise with them. *(Lily W., grade 5)*

Put down the cup and uncover the matzot.

Go forth and learn what Laban the Aramean wanted to do to our father Jacob. Pharaoh had issued a decree against the male children only, but Laban wanted to uproot everyone–as it is said:

"An Aramean wished to destroy my father; and he went down to Egypt and sojourned there, few in number; and he became there a nation – great and mighty and numerous."

"**He went down to Egypt**" forced by Divine decree.

צֵא וּלְמַד מַה בִּקֵּשׁ לָבָן הָאֲרַמִּי לַעֲשׂוֹת לְיַעֲקֹב אָבִינוּ. שֶׁפַּרְעֹה לֹא גָזַר אֶלָּא עַל הַזְּכָרִים וְלָבָן בִּקֵּשׁ לַעֲקוֹר אֶת הַכֹּל, שֶׁנֶּאֱמַר:

אֲרַמִּי אֹבֵד אָבִי, וַיֵּרֶד מִצְרַיְמָה וַיָּגָר שָׁם בִּמְתֵי מְעָט, וַיְהִי שָׁם לְגוֹי גָּדוֹל, עָצוּם וָרָב.

וַיֵּרֶד מִצְרַיְמָה -
אָנוּס עַל פִּי הַדִּבּוּר.

וַיָּגָר שָׁם -
מְלַמֵּד שֶׁלֹּא יָרַד יַעֲקֹב אָבִינוּ

42

"He sojourned there" – this teaches that our father Jacob did not go down to Egypt to settle, but only to live there temporarily. Thus it is said, "They said to Pharaoh, We have come to sojourn in the land, for there is no pasture for your servants' flocks because the hunger is severe in the land of Canaan; and now, please, let your servants dwell in the land of Goshen."

"Few in number" as it is said: "Your fathers went down to Egypt with seventy persons, and now, the Lord, your God, has made you as numerous as the stars of heaven."

"He became there a nation" this teaches that Israel was distinctive there.

"Great, mighty," as it is said: "And the children of Israel were fruitful and increased abundantly, and multiplied and became very, very mighty, and the land became filled with them."

לְהִשְׁתַּקֵּעַ בְּמִצְרַיִם אֶלָּא לָגוּר שָׁם, שֶׁנֶּאֱמַר: וַיֹּאמְרוּ אֶל פַּרְעֹה, לָגוּר בָּאָרֶץ בָּאנוּ, כִּי אֵין מִרְעֶה לַצֹּאן אֲשֶׁר לַעֲבָדֶיךָ, כִּי כָבֵד הָרָעָב בְּאֶרֶץ כְּנָעַן. וְעַתָּה יֵשְׁבוּ נָא עֲבָדֶיךָ בְּאֶרֶץ גֹּשֶׁן.

בִּמְתֵי מְעָט -

כְּמַה שֶׁנֶּאֱמַר: בְּשִׁבְעִים נֶפֶשׁ יָרְדוּ אֲבוֹתֶיךָ מִצְרָיְמָה, וְעַתָּה שָׂמְךָ יְיָ אֱלֹהֶיךָ כְּכוֹכְבֵי הַשָּׁמַיִם לָרֹב.

וַיְהִי שָׁם לְגוֹי -

מְלַמֵּד שֶׁהָיוּ יִשְׂרָאֵל מְצֻיָּנִים שָׁם.

גָּדוֹל, עָצוּם -

כְּמַה שֶׁנֶּאֱמַר: וּבְנֵי יִשְׂרָאֵל פָּרוּ וַיִּשְׁרְצוּ וַיִּרְבּוּ וַיַּעַצְמוּ בִּמְאֹד מְאֹד, וַתִּמָּלֵא הָאָרֶץ אֹתָם.

"And numerous," as it is said: "I caused you to thrive like the plants of the field, and you increased and grew and became very beautiful, your breasts developed and your hair grown long, but you were naked and bare. I passed over you and saw you wallowing in your bloods, and I said to you `By your blood you shall live,' and I said to you `By your blood you shall live!'"

"The Egyptians treated us badly and afflicted us. They put hard work upon us."

"And afflicted us," as it is said: Come, let us act cunningly with [the people] lest they multiply and, if there should be a war against us, they will join our enemies, fight against us and leave the land."

"And they made us suffer," as it is said: "They set taskmasters over [the people of Israel] to afflict them with their burdens. They built storage cities for Pharaoh, Pitom and Ramses."

וָרָב -
כְּמָה שֶׁנֶּאֱמַר: רְבָבָה כְּצֶמַח הַשָּׂדֶה נְתַתִּיךְ, וַתִּרְבִּי וַתִּגְדְּלִי וַתָּבֹאִי בַּעֲדִי עֲדָיִים, שָׁדַיִם נָכֹנוּ וּשְׂעָרֵךְ צִמֵּחַ, וְאַתְּ עֵרֹם וְעֶרְיָה. וָאֶעֱבֹר עָלַיִךְ וָאֶרְאֵךְ מִתְבּוֹסֶסֶת בְּדָמָיִךְ, וָאֹמַר לָךְ בְּדָמַיִךְ חֲיִי, וָאֹמַר לָךְ בְּדָמַיִךְ חֲיִי.

וַיָּרֵעוּ אֹתָנוּ הַמִּצְרִים וַיְעַנּוּנוּ, וַיִּתְּנוּ עָלֵינוּ עֲבֹדָה קָשָׁה.

וַיָּרֵעוּ אֹתָנוּ הַמִּצְרִים -
כְּמָה שֶׁנֶּאֱמַר: הָבָה נִתְחַכְּמָה לוֹ פֶּן יִרְבֶּה, וְהָיָה כִּי תִקְרֶאנָה מִלְחָמָה וְנוֹסַף גַּם הוּא עַל שֹׂנְאֵינוּ וְנִלְחַם בָּנוּ, וְעָלָה מִן הָאָרֶץ.

וַיְעַנּוּנוּ -
כְּמָה שֶׁנֶּאֱמַר: וַיָּשִׂימוּ עָלָיו שָׂרֵי מִסִּים לְמַעַן עַנֹּתוֹ בְּסִבְלֹתָם. וַיִּבֶן עָרֵי מִסְכְּנוֹת לְפַרְעֹה. אֶת פִּתֹם וְאֶת רַעַמְסֵס.

"And they put hard work upon us," as it is said: "The Egyptians made the children of Israel work with rigor."

וַיִּתְּנוּ עָלֵינוּ עֲבֹדָה קָשָׁה- כְּמָה שֶׁנֶּאֱמַר: וַיַּעֲבִדוּ מִצְרַיִם אֶת בְּנֵי יִשְׂרָאֵל בְּפָרֶךְ.

PERECH PEH RACH:
SILKEN SPEECH

The Rabbis play a game with the word *Perech* (backbreaking labor), breaking it down into two words—*peh rach*—soft or silken speech. Pharaoh, according to the *midrash*, began the enslavement of the Children of Israel with mild words. He proclaimed a national day of good citizenship, summoning Egyptians and foreigners alike to assemble and work to build for their country. The Hebrews, wishing, as always, to be seen as the most loyal citizens, worked tirelessly, making more bricks per capita than any other group. Their surprise was great when, the next day, all the other groups were allowed to stay home and only they were required to continue, having to match each day the prodigious total of bricks they had reached on the first day.

Harry learned to distrust those whose voices were too silken and whose promises were too unctuously offered. From the insincere offers of Voldemort to the self-serving ques-

tions of Rita Skeeter to the saccharine tones of Dolores Umbridge, he learned to judge words by their content, not their deceptive outer garb. Many have suggested that God saw to it that Moses was hampered by a speech impediment to make clear that his appeal was the message of God, not the charisma of the cult leader.

We cried out to the Lord, the God of our fathers. The Lord heard our voice, He saw our suffering, our labor and our oppression.

"We cried out to the Lord, the God of our fathers," as it is said: "During that long period, the king of Egypt died; and the children of Israel groaned because of the servitude, and they cried out. And their cry for help from their servitude rose up to God."

"The Lord heard our voice" as it said: "God heard their groaning, and God remembered His covenant with Abraham, Isaac and Jacob."

וַנִּצְעַק אֶל יְיָ אֱלֹהֵי אֲבֹתֵינוּ, וַיִּשְׁמַע יְיָ אֶת קֹלֵנוּ, וַיַּרְא אֶת עָנְיֵנוּ וְאֶת עֲמָלֵנוּ וְאֶת לַחֲצֵנוּ.

וַנִּצְעַק אֶל יְיָ אֱלֹהֵי אֲבֹתֵינוּ- כְּמָה שֶׁנֶּאֱמַר: וַיְהִי בַיָּמִים הָרַבִּים הָהֵם וַיָּמָת מֶלֶךְ מִצְרַיִם, וַיֵּאָנְחוּ בְנֵי יִשְׂרָאֵל מִן הָעֲבוֹדָה וַיִּזְעָקוּ, וַתַּעַל שַׁוְעָתָם אֶל הָאֱלֹהִים מִן הָעֲבֹדָה.

וַיִּשְׁמַע יְיָ אֶת קֹלֵנוּ - כְּמָה שֶׁנֶּאֱמַר: וַיִּשְׁמַע אֱלֹהִים אֶת נַאֲקָתָם, וַיִּזְכֹּר אֱלֹהִים אֶת בְּרִיתוֹ אֶת אַבְרָהָם, אֶת יִצְחָק וְאֶת יַעֲקֹב.

"He saw our suffering," this refers to the separation of husband and wife, as it is said: "God saw the children of Israel and God took note."

"Our labor," this refers to the "children," as it is said: "Every boy that is born, you shall throw into the river and every girl you shall keep alive."

"Our oppression," this refers to the pressure, as it is said: "I have seen the oppression with which the Egyptians oppress them."

וַיַּרְא אֶת עָנְיֵנוּ -

זוֹ פְּרִישׁוּת דֶּרֶךְ אֶרֶץ, כְּמָה שֶׁנֶּאֱמַר: וַיַּרְא אֱלֹהִים אֶת בְּנֵי יִשְׂרָאֵל וַיֵּדַע אֱלֹהִים.

וְאֶת עֲמָלֵנוּ -

אֵלּוּ הַבָּנִים. כְּמָה שֶׁנֶּאֱמַר: כָּל הַבֵּן הַיִּלּוֹד הַיְאֹרָה תַּשְׁלִיכֻהוּ וְכָל הַבַּת תְּחַיּוּן.

וְאֶת לַחֲצֵנוּ -

זֶה הַדְּחַק, כְּמָה שֶׁנֶּאֱמַר: וְגַם רָאִיתִי אֶת הַלַּחַץ אֲשֶׁר מִצְרַיִם לֹחֲצִים אֹתָם.

PERISHUT DEREKH ERETZ:
BUILDING FAMILY AT TIME OF TROUBLE

Beyond the immediate and visible threat, one of the chief dangers at a time when good is threatened by evil is the temptation faced by those fighting the overwhelming odds to despair of continu-

ing daily life in inhuman circumstances, much less bringing a new generation into the world to face the same cruelty. It takes vision, in addition to courage, to fight and plan for a better future simultaneously.

In the Exodus story, it was the women who displayed that vision. As Pharaoh's decrees demoralized the men and discouraged reproduction, the men succumbed. The women, on the other hand, joined their husbands in the fields at the end of a long day, and, with the help of their trusty mirrors, reignited the flames of romance. The midrash depicts Amram, the father of Moses and leader of his people, as divorcing his wife so as not to add to the babies being drowned by Pharoah. It was his daughter Miriam who brought him back to his senses, declaring that his decree was crueler than Pharaoh's for precluding the birth of girls, as well.

In the midst of the battle to defeat Lord Voldemort, Remus Lupin despaired of the prospect of marrying and bringing a new life into the world. He nearly abandoned his wife and unborn child to go with Harry on his quest, until Harry played the role of Miriam, firmly taking Lupin to task and refocusing him on the need to plan for posterity. It was the resulting child who survived the Battle of Hogwarts, in which his parents were killed.

The Lord took as out of Egypt with a strong hand and an outstretched arm, and with great awe, and with signs and wonders."

"The Lord took us out of Egypt," not through an angel, not through a seraph and not through a messenger. The Holy One, blessed be He, did it in His glory by Himself! Thus it is said: "In that night I will pass through the land of Egypt, and I will smite every first-born in the land of Egypt, from man to beast, and I will carry out judgments against all the gods of Egypt, I the Lord."

"I will pass through the land of Egypt," I and not an angel;

"I will smite every first-born in the land of Egypt," I and not a seraph;

"I will carry out judgments against all the gods of Egypt," I and not a messenger;

"I– the Lord," it is I, and none other!

וַיּוֹצִאֵנוּ יְיָ מִמִּצְרַיִם בְּיָד חֲזָקָה וּבִזְרֹעַ נְטוּיָה, וּבְמֹרָא גָּדֹל, וּבְאֹתוֹת וּבְמֹפְתִים.

וַיּוֹצִאֵנוּ יְיָ מִמִּצְרַיִם - לֹא עַל יְדֵי מַלְאָךְ, וְלֹא עַל יְדֵי שָׂרָף, וְלֹא עַל יְדֵי שָׁלִיחַ, אֶלָּא הַקָּדוֹשׁ בָּרוּךְ הוּא בִּכְבוֹדוֹ וּבְעַצְמוֹ, שֶׁנֶּאֱמַר: וְעָבַרְתִּי בְאֶרֶץ מִצְרַיִם בַּלַּיְלָה הַזֶּה, וְהִכֵּיתִי כָל בְּכוֹר בְּאֶרֶץ מִצְרַיִם מֵאָדָם וְעַד בְּהֵמָה, וּבְכָל אֱלֹהֵי מִצְרַיִם אֶעֱשֶׂה שְׁפָטִים. אֲנִי יְיָ.

וְעָבַרְתִּי בְאֶרֶץ מִצְרַיִם בַּלַּיְלָה הַזֶּה - אֲנִי וְלֹא מַלְאָךְ

וְהִכֵּיתִי כָל בְּכוֹר בְּאֶרֶץ מִצְרַיִם - אֲנִי וְלֹא שָׂרָף

וּבְכָל אֱלֹהֵי מִצְרַיִם אֶעֱשֶׂה שְׁפָטִים - אֲנִי ולֹא הַשָּׁלִיחַ.

אֲנִי יְיָ - אֲנִי הוּא ולֹא אַחֵר.

LO AL YEDEI MAL'AKH:
SHEDDING INTERMEDIARIES AND SHIELDS

⚡

"It's got to be me," Harry says at the final showdown. "But Potter doesn't mean that," Voldemort rejoins. He taunts Harry, claiming that Harry hid behind the skirts of others and allowed them to fight his battles and die in his place.

But Harry is prepared. "There are no more Horcruxes. It's just you and me."

This was the moment when Harry, who had sought a father throughout the seven books, became the father he sought. It was the moment when, after the death of Dumbledore, arguably the Godlike figure of the series, Harry takes his place and personally steps up to fight the ultimate evil. It is the culmination of his development, when all that he had learned about the world and himself came together.

Harry's moment echoes the instant of the Biblical plague of the smiting of the firstborn Egyptians. As the Haggadah emphasizes, the time for agents is past. The time for an Aaron to strike the water or a Moses to target the heavens is over. When it comes time to reveal the face of ultimate good and finally vanquish evil and its supporters, God says, *"Ani hu v'lo acher."* It's got to be me.

"With a strong hand," this refers to the dever (pestilence) as it is said: "Behold, the hand of the Lord will be upon your livestock in the field, upon the horses, the donkeys, the camels, the herds and the flocks, a very severe pestilence."

"With an outstretched arm," this refers to the sword, as it is said: "His sword was drawn, in his hand, stretched out over Jerusalem."

"With great awe," this refers to the revelation of the Shekhinah (Divine Presence), as it is said: "Has any God ever tried to take for himself a nation from the midst of another nation, with trials, signs and wonders, with war and with a strong hand and an outstretched arm, and with great manifestations, like all that the Lord your God, did for you in Egypt before your eyes!"

"With signs," this refers to the staff, as it is said: "Take in your hand this staff with which you shall perform the signs."

בְּיָד חֲזָקָה -

זוֹ הַדֶּבֶר, כְּמָה שֶׁנֶּאֱמַר: הִנֵּה יַד יְיָ הוֹיָה בְּמִקְנְךָ אֲשֶׁר בַּשָּׂדֶה, בַּסּוּסִים, בַּחֲמֹרִים, בַּגְּמַלִּים, בַּבָּקָר וּבַצֹּאן, דֶּבֶר כָּבֵד מְאֹד.

וּבִזְרֹעַ נְטוּיָה -

זוֹ הַחֶרֶב, כְּמָה שֶׁנֶּאֱמַר: וְחַרְבּוֹ שְׁלוּפָה בְּיָדוֹ, נְטוּיָה עַל יְרוּשָׁלָיִם.

בְּמֹרָא גָּדֹל -

זוֹ גִּלּוּי שְׁכִינָה, כְּמָה שֶׁנֶּאֱמַר: אוֹ הֲנִסָּה אֱלֹהִים לָבֹא לָקַחַת לוֹ גוֹי מִקֶּרֶב גּוֹי בְּמַסֹּת בְּאֹתֹת וּבְמוֹפְתִים, וּבְמִלְחָמָה וּבְיָד חֲזָקָה וּבִזְרֹעַ נְטוּיָה, וּבְמוֹרָאִים גְּדֹלִים, כְּכֹל אֲשֶׁר עָשָׂה לָכֶם יְיָ אֱלֹהֵיכֶם בְּמִצְרַיִם לְעֵינֶיךָ.

וּבְאֹתוֹת -

זֶה הַמַּטֶּה, כְּמָה שֶׁנֶּאֱמַר: וְאֶת הַמַּטֶּה הַזֶּה תִּקַּח בְּיָדְךָ, אֲשֶׁר תַּעֲשֶׂה בּוֹ אֶת הָאֹתֹת. "

"And wonders," this refers to the blood, as it is said: "And I shall show wonders in heaven and on earth.

וּבְמֹפְתִים - זֶה הַדָּם, כְּמָה שֶׁנֶּאֱמַר: וְנָתַתִּי מוֹפְתִים בַּשָּׁמַיִם וּבָאָרֶץ,

As each of the following words is said, remove a little wine from the cup, with the finger or by pouring.

Blood and fire, and pillars of smoke.

דָּם וָאֵשׁ וְתִימְרוֹת עָשָׁן.

WAND AND STAFF... AND FEATHER

On the surface, the staff of Moses would seem to directly parallel the wand of Harry Potter. God instructed Moses to "take this staff in your hand through which you shall perform the signs." In fact, the *midrash* depicts the staff as having the acronym of the the ten plagues inscribed upon it. The wizard, of course, channeled all of his magic through the wand that "chose" him.

But there is a major difference. Whereas the greatest wizard would be rendered powerless in the absence of a wand, such was not the case with the staff of Moses. When he waited the split second extra, Dumbledore was disarmed by Draco Malfoy in the Astronomy Tower and was indeed unable to defend himself. Moses, on the other hand, undergoes a pro-

cess in which God helps him learn that it is not the wand but the will of God that metes out plagues. In the plagues of hail and locusts, (numbers 7 and 8), God instructs him to initiate the plague by "stretching forth his hand." Moses, however, stretches forth his staff to achieve the same effect. It is only in the ninth plague, that of darkness, that Moses stretches forth his hand and, lo and behold, discovers that the staff was only a prop, after all, more akin to the feather that Dumbo the elephant discovered was no longer the secret of his ability to fly.

Another interpretation of Deuteronomy 26:8 is: "strong hand" indicates two plagues; "out-stretched arm" indicates two more plagues; "great awe" indicates two plagues; "signs" indicates two more plagues; and "wonders" two more plagues.

This then is a total of ten plagues that the Holy One blessed be He brought upon the Egyptians in Egypt, and they are as follows:

דָּבָר אַחֵר: בְּיָד חֲזָקָה - שְׁתַּיִם, וּבִזְרֹעַ נְטוּיָה - שְׁתַּיִם, וּבְמֹרָא גָּדֹל - שְׁתַּיִם, וּבְאֹתוֹת - שְׁתַּיִם, וּבְמֹפְתִים - שְׁתַּיִם.

אֵלּוּ עֶשֶׂר מַכּוֹת שֶׁהֵבִיא הַקָּדוֹשׁ בָּרוּךְ הוּא עַל הַמִּצְרִים בְּמִצְרַיִם, וְאֵלּוּ הֵן:

Remove a drop of wine for each plague.

Blood, Frogs, Lice,
Beasts, Pestilence,
Boils, Hail, Locusts,
Darkness,
Death of First Born.

דָּם, צְפַרְדֵּעַ, כִּנִּים,
עָרוֹב, דֶּבֶר,
שְׁחִין, בָּרָד, אַרְבֶּה,
חֹשֶׁךְ,
מַכַּת בְּכוֹרוֹת.

Remove a drop of wine for each abbreviation.

Rabbi Yehuda would assign the plagues three mnemonic signs:

Detzakh, Adash, B'Ahav.

רַבִּי יְהוּדָה הָיָה נוֹתֵן בָּהֶם
סִמָּנִים:
דְּצַ"ךְ עֲדַ"שׁ בְּאַחַ"ב.

Student Voices - מתלמידי יותר מכולם

What is the best punishment you or a friend ever received?

★ **No screens for an hour.** *(Roni C., grade 8)*
★ **A time-out and getting yelled at.** *(Dahlia A., grade 8)*
★ **Knowing I made others feel bad.** *(Noa I., grade 8)*

10 PLAGUES:
PUNISHMENTS AND EDUCATION

When Rabbi Yehuda converts the plagues into an acrostic—*Detzakh, Adash, B'Ahav*—it is not merely a sacred mnemonic, ROY G BIV with a *kipah*. Many commentaries identify patterns in the plagues that work out according to these groupings. One such pattern, put forth by Rabbi Meir Leib Malbim, explains that plagues 3, 6, and 9 are not preceded by warning, while the others are. His reason: in each set of three, the first two aim to teach Pharaoh a particular lesson, while the third is meant to punish him for not having learned that lesson. In other words, in at least six of the first nine plagues, what looks like a punishment is actually education.

At Hogwarts, among the seamier instructors, the exact opposite is true. The sadistic pronouncements of Dolores Umbridge are an exercise in asserting a power structure. While she would describe them as teaching a lesson, Harry's wounded hand would beg to differ. A lesson in Potions, even while teaching, often devolved into an exercise in humiliation. The Exodus story reminds us that even when punishment is unavoidable, honoring the image of God means educating even when forced to punish.

THE BLOOD OF
LIFE AND DEATH

At first glance we would classify blood as a symbol of death. When Moses twice turns water to blood the message is clear—he has been authorized to turn life into death. When Voldemort hides a horcrux, he insists on a sampling of blood to access its portal. Even the unicorn blood that he drank to stay alive could only assure him an accursed life.

But a closer look reveals a variety of blood that is the agent of life, and that is the blood of sacrifice. Harry's mother gave her life to protect her son and her magical protection rested in Harry's blood. For that reason, when Voldemort used Harry's blood to enable his return, he assured himself of never being able to possess Harry, and later, Harry's identical sacrifice protected all of Hogwarts. The *midrash* on this line of the Haggadah, present only in some editions, explains the plural form of the word, literally "through your *bloods* you shall live," by pointing to two commandments which involved sacrifice and guaranteed the passage of the Children of Israel from Egypt. The Paschal Sacrifice (*Korban Pesach*) and the commandment of circumcision (*Brit Milah*) symbolize the potency of self sacrifice and the positive aspect of the blood of life.

DETZAKH, ADASH, B'AHAV:
ON THE POWER OF ACRONYMS

Words are powerful. According to the *mishna* (*Avot* 5:1), the world was brought into being through God's ten statements. In Egypt, that creation was deconstructed through the ten plagues. What could be stronger than ten statements of creation? According to Rabbi Yehuda, the answer is not ten plagues, but three abbreviations. It is as if the power of the words is distilled into the concentrated form of the abbreviations. As mentioned above, a *midrashic* tradition maintains that the abbreviations were actually inscribed on the staff of Moses.

Abbreviations in Harry Potter, like so much else, are both meaningful and playful. They demonstrate how J.K. Rowling can make a point, yet simultaneously poke fun at it so as not to appear overly preachy or earnest. If labeling wizarding SAT or GRE exams the OWLs and NEWTs were not enough, the most overt attempt at preaching "human" rights, Hermione's campaign on behalf of house elves, is denoted by the impossible-to-say-with-a-straight-face acronym S.P.E.W. These abbreviations, too, have power, but the power of humor, which, in the right measure, can be an agent of creation too.

What is your favorite abbreviation, in English or in Hebrew?

★ תרי"ג ★ רש"י ★ אע"פ ★ זמ"ן נק"ט ★ דצ"ך עד"ש באח"ב ★ ב"ה

★ OMG! ★ LOL ★ SCUBA ★ YOLO ★ IDK ★ NFL
★ MLB
★ ILYSM [I love you so much] *(Rena S., grade 6)*
★ IDIC [Infinite Diversity Infinite Combinations] *(Avi C., grade 7)*
★ Abbrev. *(Davidi H., grade 7)*

Rabbi Yose the Galilean says: How does one derive that, after the ten plagues in Egypt, the Egyptians suffered fifty plagues at the Sea? Concerning the plagues in Egypt the Torah states that "the magicians said to Pharaoh, it is the *finger* of God." However, at the Sea, the Torah relates that "Israel saw the great *hand* which the Lord manifested in Egypt. The people revered the Lord.

רַבִּי יוֹסֵי הַגְּלִילִי אוֹמֵר: מִנַּיִן אַתָּה אוֹמֵר שֶׁלָּקוּ הַמִּצְרִים בְּמִצְרַיִם עֶשֶׂר מַכּוֹת וְעַל הַיָּם לָקוּ חֲמִשִּׁים מַכּוֹת? בְּמִצְרַיִם מָה הוּא אוֹמֵר? וַיֹּאמְרוּ הַחַרְטֻמִּים אֶל פַּרְעֹה: אֶצְבַּע אֱלֹהִים הוּא. וְעַל הַיָּם מָה הוּא אוֹמֵר? וַיַּרְא יִשְׂרָאֵל אֶת הַיָּד הַגְּדֹלָה אֲשֶׁר עָשָׂה יְיָ בְּמִצְרַיִם, וַיִּירְאוּ הָעָם אֶת יְיָ, וַיַּאֲמִינוּ בַּייָ וּבְמֹשֶׁה עַבְדּוֹ.

They believed in the Lord and in Moses, His servant." If in Egypt they were struck with ten plagues through (merely) the "finger" (of God), you can extrapolate that at the sea (where they experienced His "hand,") they were struck with fifty plagues.

כַּמָּה לָקוּ בְאֶצְבַּע? עֶשֶׂר מַכּוֹת. אֱמוֹר מֵעַתָּה: בְּמִצְרַיִם לָקוּ עֶשֶׂר מַכּוֹת וְעַל הַיָּם לָקוּ חֲמִשִּׁים מַכּוֹת.

ויאמינו בה׳ ובמשה עבדו
THEY BELIEVED IN GOD AND IN MOSES, HIS SERVANT

This is the only occurrence of the name of Moses in the entire Haggadah. The most popular reason given for the absence of Moses's name, despite the important role he played in the Exodus, is that the Haggadah wishes to emphasize the centrality of God's involvement in the story (See Lo al Yedei Mal'akh above), as well as the self-effacing nature of Moses. Moses becomes "He-Who-Must-Not-Be-Named," not from fear as in the case of Lord Voldemort, but as an indicator of humility. He recedes to the background, allowing God to be He-Who-Must-Be-Named.

Student Voices - מתלמידי יותר מכולם

What is the place where you are the happiest, your "happy place"?

★ Israel.
★ Camp.
★ My room.
★ The Beach.
★ My grandparents house.
★ Anywhere with my friends.
★ On stage performing. *(Dafna H., grade 8)*
★ Scuba Diving. *(Gabriel S., grade 8)*
★ Snowboarding. *(Avi T. , grade 8)*
★ Basketball court. *(Noam S., grade 8)*
★ The squishy chair in my room with a book. *(Sadie L, grade 7)*
★ My cheerleading gym. *(Chana J., grade 5)*
★ My singing teacher's music room. *(Talia S., grade 5)*

Rabbi Eliezer says: How does one derive that every plague that God inflicted upon the Egyptians in in Egypt was comprised of four plagues? It is written: "He sent upon them his fierce anger, wrath, fury and trouble, a band of evil messengers." Since each plague was comprised of 1) wrath, 2) fury, 3) trouble and 4) a band of evil messengers, they must have suffered forty plagues in Egypt and two hundred at the Sea.

Rabbi Akiva says: How does one derive that every plague that God inflicted upon the Egyptians in in Egypt was comprised of five plagues? It is written: "He sent upon them his fierce anger, wrath, fury and trouble, a band of evil messengers." Since each plague was comprised of 1) fierce anger 2) wrath 3) fury 4) trouble and 5) a band of evil messengers, they must have suffered fifty plagues in Egypt and two hundred and fifty at the Sea.

רַבִּי אֱלִיעֶזֶר אוֹמֵר: מִנַּיִן שֶׁכָּל מַכָּה וּמַכָּה שֶׁהֵבִיא הַקָּדוֹשׁ בָּרוּךְ הוּא עַל הַמִּצְרִים בְּמִצְרַיִם הָיְתָה שֶׁל אַרְבַּע מַכּוֹת? שֶׁנֶּאֱמַר: יְשַׁלַּח בָּם חֲרוֹן אַפּוֹ, עֶבְרָה וָזַעַם וְצָרָה, מִשְׁלַחַת מַלְאֲכֵי רָעִים. עֶבְרָה - אַחַת, וָזַעַם - שְׁתַּיִם, וְצָרָה - שָׁלֹשׁ, מִשְׁלַחַת מַלְאֲכֵי רָעִים - אַרְבַּע. אֱמוֹר מֵעַתָּה: בְּמִצְרַיִם לָקוּ אַרְבָּעִים מַכּוֹת וְעַל הַיָּם לָקוּ מָאתַיִם מַכּוֹת.

רַבִּי עֲקִיבָא אוֹמֵר: מִנַּיִן שֶׁכָּל מַכָּה וּמַכָּה שֶׁהֵבִיא הַקָּדוֹשׁ בָּרוּךְ הוּא עַל הַמִּצְרִים בְּמִצְרַיִם הָיְתָה שֶׁל חָמֵשׁ מַכּוֹת? שֶׁנֶּאֱמַר: יְשַׁלַּח בָּם חֲרוֹן אַפּוֹ, עֶבְרָה וָזַעַם וְצָרָה, מִשְׁלַחַת מַלְאֲכֵי רָעִים. חֲרוֹן אַפּוֹ- אַחַת, עֶבְרָה - שְׁתַּיִם, וָזַעַם - שָׁלֹשׁ, וְצָרָה - אַרְבַּע, מִשְׁלַחַת מַלְאֲכֵי רָעִים - חָמֵשׁ. אֱמוֹר מֵעַתָּה: בְּמִצְרַיִם לָקוּ חֲמִשִּׁים מַכּוֹת וְעַל הַיָּם לָקוּ חֲמִשִּׁים וּמָאתַיִם מַכּוֹת.

God has bestowed so many favors upon us!

Had He brought us out of Egypt, and not executed judgments against the Egyptians, It would have been enough!

Had He executed judgments against the Egyptians, and not their gods, It would have been enough!

Had He executed judgments against their gods and not put to death their firstborn, It would have been enough!

Had He put to death their firstborn, and not given us their riches, It would have been enough!

Had He given us their riches, and not split the Sea for us, It would have been enough!

Had He split the Sea for us, and not led us through it on dry land, It would have been enough!

Had He led us through it on dry land, and not sunk our foes in it, It would have been enough!

כַּמָּה מַעֲלוֹת טוֹבוֹת לַמָּקוֹם עָלֵינוּ!

אִלּוּ הוֹצִיאָנוּ מִמִּצְרַיִם וְלֹא עָשָׂה בָהֶם שְׁפָטִים, **דַּיֵּנוּ.**

אִלּוּ עָשָׂה בָהֶם שְׁפָטִים, וְלֹא עָשָׂה בֵאלֹהֵיהֶם, **דַּיֵּנוּ.**

אִלּוּ עָשָׂה בֵאלֹהֵיהֶם, וְלֹא הָרַג אֶת בְּכוֹרֵיהֶם, **דַּיֵּנוּ.**

אִלּוּ הָרַג אֶת בְּכוֹרֵיהֶם וְלֹא נָתַן לָנוּ אֶת מָמוֹנָם, **דַּיֵּנוּ.**

אִלּוּ נָתַן לָנוּ אֶת מָמוֹנָם וְלֹא קָרַע לָנוּ אֶת הַיָּם, **דַּיֵּנוּ.**

אִלּוּ קָרַע לָנוּ אֶת הַיָּם וְלֹא הֶעֱבִירָנוּ בְתוֹכוֹ בֶּחָרָבָה, **דַּיֵּנוּ.**

אִלּוּ הֶעֱבִירָנוּ בְתוֹכוֹ בֶּחָרָבָה וְלֹא שִׁקַּע צָרֵנוּ בְּתוֹכוֹ, **דַּיֵּנוּ.**

Had He sunk our foes in it, and not satisfied our needs in the desert for forty years, It would have been enough!

Had He satisfied our needs in the desert for forty years, and not fed us the manna, It would have been enough!

Had He fed us the manna, and not given us the Sabbath, It would have been enough!
Had He given us the Sabbath, and not brought us to Mount Sinai, It would have been enough!

Had He brought us to Mount Sinai, and not given us the To-rah, It would have been enough!

Had He given us the Torah, and not brought us into Israel, It would have been enough!

Had He brought us into Israel, and not built the Temple for us, It would have been enough!

אִלּוּ שִׁקַּע צָרֵנוּ בְּתוֹכוֹ וְלֹא סִפֵּק צָרְכֵּנוּ בַּמִּדְבָּר אַרְבָּעִים שָׁנָה,
דַּיֵּינוּ.

אִלּוּ סִפֵּק צָרְכֵּנוּ בַּמִּדְבָּר אַרְבָּעִים שָׁנָה וְלֹא הֶאֱכִילָנוּ אֶת הַמָּן,
דַּיֵּינוּ.

אִלּוּ הֶאֱכִילָנוּ אֶת הַמָּן וְלֹא נָתַן לָנוּ אֶת הַשַּׁבָּת,
דַּיֵּינוּ.

אִלּוּ נָתַן לָנוּ אֶת הַשַּׁבָּת, וְלֹא קֵרְבָנוּ לִפְנֵי הַר סִינַי,
דַּיֵּינוּ.

אִלּוּ קֵרְבָנוּ לִפְנֵי הַר סִינַי, וְלֹא נָתַן לָנוּ אֶת הַתּוֹרָה,
דַּיֵּינוּ.

אִלּוּ נָתַן לָנוּ אֶת הַתּוֹרָה וְלֹא הִכְנִיסָנוּ לְאֶרֶץ יִשְׂרָאֵל,
דַּיֵּינוּ.

אִלּוּ הִכְנִיסָנוּ לְאֶרֶץ יִשְׂרָאֵל וְלֹא בָנָה לָנוּ אֶת בֵּית הַבְּחִירָה,
דַּיֵּינוּ.

HAD HE BROUGHT US TO HAR SINAI:
THE INFLUENCE OF PLACE

How we can say that had God brought us to Sinai without giving us the Torah, it would have been sufficient? Isn't that the equivalent of being all dressed up with no place to go? Wasn't the entire purpose of arriving at Sinai to receive the Torah? One answer suggested is that places have an effect upon us. We each have our "happy place." For some it may be a vacation spot, for others a room in their home, and, for the very fortunate, their places of work or prayer may also be their places of greatest joy and fulfillment. Sinai was such a place for the Children of Israel. It was where they coalesced as a people and experienced unity under the protection of God. The Talmud says that when they reached Sinai, they were purified from the spiritual taint of the sin of the Garden of Eden. They were ready for a new beginning.

Hogwarts was home for both Harry and Voldemort. As orphans whose "real" home was a place of torment, they made school their happy place. As part of that relationship, they explored more of the castle and the grounds than any of their contemporaries, finding chambers of secrets, rooms of requirement, and venturing far beyond the conventional bounds of their respective houses. Is it any wonder that

Voldemort chose Hogwarts as the location for one of his horcruxes or that, even when he had turned against the Head-master, he still would have accepted a teaching position, had it been offered? In fact, the Battle of Hogwarts was really, in the end, also to decide who was the tenant and who was the landlord of Hogwarts.

Since God did so many great favors for us, we should be so much more grateful! He brought us out of Egypt, exe-cuted judgments against the Egyptians, executed judgments against their gods, put to death their firstborn, gave us their riches, split the Sea for us, led us through it on dry land, sank our foes in it, satisfied our needs in the desert for forty years, fed us the manna, gave us the Sabbath, brought us to Mount Sinai, gave us the Torah, brought us into Israel and built the Temple for us to atone for all of our sins!

עַל אַחַת, כַּמָּה וְכַמָּה, טוֹבָה כְּפוּלָה וּמְכֻפֶּלֶת לַמָּקוֹם עָלֵינוּ: שֶׁהוֹצִיאָנוּ מִמִּצְרַיִם, וְעָשָׂה בָהֶם שְׁפָטִים, וְעָשָׂה בֵאלֹהֵיהֶם, וְהָרַג אֶת בְּכוֹרֵיהֶם, וְנָתַן לָנוּ אֶת מָמוֹנָם, וְקָרַע לָנוּ אֶת הַיָּם, וְהֶעֱבִירָנוּ בְתוֹכוֹ בֶּחָרָבָה, וְשִׁקַּע צָרֵנוּ בְּתוֹכוֹ, וְסִפֵּק צָרְכֵּנוּ בַּמִּדְבָּר אַרְבָּעִים שָׁנָה, וְהֶאֱכִילָנוּ אֶת הַמָּן, וְנָתַן לָנוּ אֶת הַשַּׁבָּת, וְקֵרְבָנוּ לִפְנֵי הַר סִינַי, וְנָתַן לָנוּ אֶת הַתּוֹרָה, וְהִכְנִיסָנוּ לְאֶרֶץ יִשְׂרָאֵל, וּבָנָה לָנוּ אֶת בֵּית הַבְּחִירָה לְכַפֵּר עַל כָּל עֲוֹנוֹתֵינוּ.

Rabban Gamliel would teach: Anyone who has not spoken of three things on Passover has not fulfilled their obligation, and these three things are:

The Pascal Lamb, Matzah, and Maror

The Pesah which our ancestors ate when the Second Temple stood: What is the reason for it? They ate the Pesah because the Holy One, Blessed be He "passed over" the houses of our ancestors in Egypt, as it is written: "You shall say, 'It is the Passover offering for God, who passed over the houses of the Israelites, as he struck the Egyptians, but saved our homes. The people kneeled and bowed down.

רַבָּן גַּמְלִיאֵל הָיָה אוֹמֵר: כָּל שֶׁלֹּא אָמַר שְׁלֹשָׁה דְבָרִים אֵלּוּ בַּפֶּסַח, לֹא יָצָא יְדֵי חוֹבָתוֹ, וְאֵלּוּ הֵן:

פֶּסַח, מַצָּה, וּמָרוֹר.

פֶּסַח שֶׁהָיוּ אֲבוֹתֵינוּ אוֹכְלִים בִּזְמַן שֶׁבֵּית הַמִּקְדָּשׁ הָיָה קַיָּם, עַל שׁוּם מָה? עַל שׁוּם שֶׁפָּסַח הַקָּדוֹשׁ בָּרוּךְ הוּא עַל בָּתֵּי אֲבוֹתֵינוּ בְּמִצְרַיִם, שֶׁנֶּאֱמַר: וַאֲמַרְתֶּם זֶבַח פֶּסַח הוּא לַיי, אֲשֶׁר פָּסַח עַל בָּתֵּי בְנֵי יִשְׂרָאֵל בְּמִצְרַיִם בְּנָגְפּוֹ אֶת מִצְרַיִם, וְאֶת בָּתֵּינוּ הִצִּיל, וַיִּקֹּד הָעָם וַיִּשְׁתַּחֲווּ.

PESACH:
WILLINGNESS TO SACRIFICE
SELF-SACRIFICE

When the time came for the Israelites to leave Egypt, they didn't have the exit ticket. The *midrash* portrays them as lacking the necessary personal merits to be deserving of the Exodus. Here too, God, in his in his kindness, provided them with opportunities to earn redemption. The *mitzvah* explicitly mentioned in the Torah is the Paschal sacrifice. The Rabbis are quick to point out that it was risky to sacrifice an animal worshipped by the Egyptians in the midst of the land of Egypt. The Jews had to take that risk. The Rabbis add the *mitzvah* of circumcision, which also demands physical sacrifice of one's own flesh.

Self-sacrifice is the crux upon which the entire Hogwarts epic rests. It was Lily Potter's self-sacrifice to save her son which provided him the protection, the tools, and the example he needed to survive and ultimately defeat Voldemort. (See my essay and song on Chad Gadya to trace the chain, step by step.) This explanation of *korban*, or sacrifice, fits well with the view of the Ramban (Nachmanides) that the symbolism of animal sacrifice is the self-sacrifice of the person who brings the offering.

Pick up or point to the matzah and say:

This Matzah which we eat, what is its reason? It is because there was insufficient time for the dough of our ancestors to rise when the Holy One, Blessed be He revealed Himself to us and redeemed us, as it is written: "They baked the dough which they had brought forth from Egypt into cakes of unleavened bread because it had not risen, for having been driven out of Egypt they could not tarry. Neither had they made any provisions for themselves."

מַצָּה זוֹ שֶׁאָנוּ אוֹכְלִים, עַל שׁוּם מָה? עַל שׁוּם שֶׁלֹּא הִסְפִּיק בְּצֵקָם שֶׁל אֲבוֹתֵינוּ לְהַחֲמִיץ עַד שֶׁנִּגְלָה עֲלֵיהֶם מֶלֶךְ מַלְכֵי הַמְּלָכִים, הַקָּדוֹשׁ בָּרוּךְ הוּא, וּגְאָלָם, שֶׁנֶּאֱמַר: וַיֹּאפוּ אֶת הַבָּצֵק אֲשֶׁר הוֹצִיאוּ מִמִּצְרַיִם עֻגֹת מַצּוֹת, כִּי לֹא חָמֵץ, כִּי גֹרְשׁוּ מִמִּצְרַיִם וְלֹא יָכְלוּ לְהִתְמַהְמֵהַּ, וְגַם צֵדָה לֹא עָשׂוּ לָהֶם.

MATZAH: SPEED AND HASTE
NO SUBSTITUTE FOR SPEED

Matzah reminds us that there is sometimes no substitute for speed. The entire baking process must be completed within 18 minutes or else what might have been Matzah (מצה) becomes Hametz (חמץ). A famous observation notes that the difference between the two Hebrew words, which share two

letters, is the tiny line which connects the leg and roof of the letter hay, transforming it into a het. It's the split second in the baking of the matzah or the timing of the lighting of candles amidst the Friday afternoon rush that determines whether an act is a *mitzvah* or, God forbid, a sin. The speed of Pesach is a reflection of the speed of the Exodus, which is preserved by the Torah in the term *hipazon*: "For you left Egypt in a state of *hipazon*…"

Speed is also an essential element in the Harry Potter novels. We discussed above how events tend to hurtle past, sometimes even needing to be slowed down, in order to allow for precision timing. But speed is significant in its own right. It is in the flight of an owl carrying an urgent message, and in the bumpy aerial path of the Weasleys' enchanted car, plummeting into the Whomping Willow. It is in the contrast drawn between the exasperatingly deliberate life of the centaurs and the frenetic pace of humanity. But most of all it is in Quidditch. Harry finds freedom in flight. As he soars, he throws off the shackles of orphanhood, Mugglehood, and victimhood. In the air, he is in control and no one can catch him...or so he thinks. It is no accident that Voldemort, who has so many connections to Harry, shares the thrill of flight and speed. The ability that stands out in Book Seven is Voldemort's capacity to fly without a broomstick. And yet, at the moment that he seeks to conquer Harry in Harry's own domain, when he discerns the "real" Harry flying with Hagrid on the way to Shell Cottage, his wand betrays him and Harry's mastery of the air remains unsurpassed.

Pick up or point to the maror, and say:

This Maror – why do we eat it? For the Egyptians embittered the lives of our ancestors in Egypt, as the verse says: "They embittered their lives with hard labor, with mortar and bricks, and with every form of work in the field, all of their backbreaking labors which they forced them to perform."

מָרוֹר זֶה שֶׁאָנוּ אוֹכְלִים, עַל שׁוּם מָה? עַל שׁוּם שֶׁמֵּרְרוּ הַמִּצְרִים אֶת חַיֵּי אֲבוֹתֵינוּ בְּמִצְרַיִם, שֶׁנֶּאֱמַר: וַיְמָרְרוּ אֶת חַיֵּיהֶם בַּעֲבֹדָה קָשָׁה, בְּחֹמֶר וּבִלְבֵנִים וּבְכָל עֲבֹדָה בַּשָּׂדֶה אֶת כָּל עֲבֹדָתָם אֲשֶׁר עָבְדוּ בָהֶם בְּפָרֶךְ.

BITTERNESS: WHERE DO YOU PUT IT?

Harry had much bitterness in his life. Deprived of his parents as a young child, his life at the Dursleys was misery. At Hogwarts, he was the target of both students and teachers through no fault of his own. And, of course, he was in constant life-threatening peril from the man who had killed his from the man who killed his parents. If anyone had the right to feel embittered, it was Harry. And yet he showed that you can experience bitterness without becoming embittered. You can take the lessons of your suffering and use them to

appreciate your blessings and spare others suffering. Voldemort and Snape would have done well to learn this lesson from Harry.

This lesson is implicit in how we experience the bitter herb, the maror, at the Seder. We recognize the importance of re-experiencing the bitterness of servitude, but always in context. On the Seder plate, in the list of Rabban Gamliel, in the *Korekh* sandwich, *maror* is bracketed by the symbols of freedom, teaching us that bitterness can be used as a prelude to sweetness and can ultimately be used to spare others what we have suffered.

In every generation, each person must feel as if he or she had personally left Egypt, as it says, "Tell your child on that day, 'For the sake of this God did (miracles) for me when I left Egypt.'" God redeemed not only our ancestors, but redeemed us along with them, as the Torah says: "He took us out from there, in order to bring us (to Israel) to give us the land that He promised our ancestors."

בְּכָל דּוֹר וָדוֹר חַיָּב אָדָם לִרְאוֹת אֶת עַצְמוֹ כְּאִלּוּ הוּא יָצָא מִמִּצְרַיִם, שֶׁנֶּאֱמַר: וְהִגַּדְתָּ לְבִנְךָ בַּיּוֹם הַהוּא לֵאמֹר, בַּעֲבוּר זֶה עָשָׂה יְיָ לִי בְּצֵאתִי מִמִּצְרָיִם. לֹא אֶת אֲבוֹתֵינוּ בִּלְבָד גָּאַל הַקָּדוֹשׁ בָּרוּךְ הוּא, אֶלָּא אַף אוֹתָנוּ גָּאַל עִמָּהֶם, שֶׁנֶּאֱמַר: וְאוֹתָנוּ הוֹצִיא מִשָּׁם, לְמַעַן הָבִיא אֹתָנוּ, לָתֶת לָנוּ אֶת הָאָרֶץ אֲשֶׁר נִשְׁבַּע לַאֲבֹתֵנוּ.

Cover the matzah, raise the cup of wine and say:

Therefore it is our duty to thank and praise, pay tribute and glorify, exalt and honor, bless and acclaim the One who performed all these miracles for our ancestors and for us. He took us out of slavery into freedom, out of grief into joy, out of mourning into a festival, out of darkness into a great light, out of slavery into redemption. We will recite a new song before Him! Halleluyah.

Praise the Lord! Praise, you servants of the Lord, praise the name of the Lord. Blessed be the name of the Lord from this time forth and forever. From the rising of the sun to its setting, the Lord's name is to be praised. High above all nations is the Lord; above the heavens is His glory. Who is like the Lord our God, who though enthroned on high, lowers himself to look down upon heaven and earth? He raises the poor man out of the dust and lifts the needy one out of the trash heap, to seat them with nobles, with the nobles of His people. He turns the barren wife into a happy mother of children. Halleluyah!

לְפִיכָךְ אֲנַחְנוּ חַיָּבִים לְהוֹדוֹת, לְהַלֵּל, לְשַׁבֵּחַ, לְפָאֵר, לְרוֹמֵם, לְהַדֵּר, לְבָרֵךְ, לְעַלֵּה וּלְקַלֵּס לְמִי שֶׁעָשָׂה לַאֲבוֹתֵינוּ וְלָנוּ אֶת כָּל הַנִּסִּים הָאֵלּוּ: הוֹצִיאָנוּ מֵעַבְדוּת לְחֵרוּת מִיָּגוֹן לְשִׂמְחָה, וּמֵאֵבֶל לְיוֹם טוֹב, וּמֵאֲפֵלָה לְאוֹר גָּדוֹל, וּמִשִּׁעְבּוּד לִגְאֻלָּה. וְנֹאמַר לְפָנָיו שִׁירָה חֲדָשָׁה: הַלְלוּיָהּ.

הַלְלוּ יָהּ הַלְלוּ עַבְדֵי יְהֹוָה הַלְלוּ אֶת שֵׁם יְהֹוָה. יְהִי שֵׁם יְהֹוָה מְבֹרָךְ מֵעַתָּה וְעַד עוֹלָם. מִמִּזְרַח שֶׁמֶשׁ עַד מְבוֹאוֹ מְהֻלָּל שֵׁם יְהֹוָה. רָם עַל כָּל גּוֹיִם יְהֹוָה עַל הַשָּׁמַיִם כְּבוֹדוֹ. מִי כַּיהֹוָה אֱלֹהֵינוּ הַמַּגְבִּיהִי לָשָׁבֶת. הַמַּשְׁפִּילִי לִרְאוֹת בַּשָּׁמַיִם וּבָאָרֶץ. מְקִימִי מֵעָפָר דָּל מֵאַשְׁפֹּת יָרִים אֶבְיוֹן. לְהוֹשִׁיבִי עִם נְדִיבִים עִם נְדִיבֵי עַמּוֹ. מוֹשִׁיבִי עֲקֶרֶת הַבַּיִת אֵם הַבָּנִים שְׂמֵחָה הַלְלוּ יָהּ.

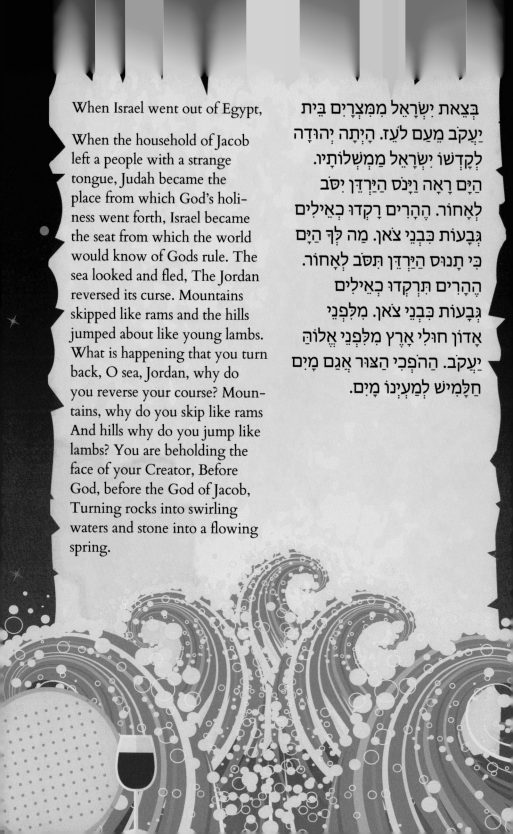

When Israel went out of Egypt,

When the household of Jacob left a people with a strange tongue, Judah became the place from which God's holiness went forth, Israel became the seat from which the world would know of Gods rule. The sea looked and fled, The Jordan reversed its curse. Mountains skipped like rams and the hills jumped about like young lambs. What is happening that you turn back, O sea, Jordan, why do you reverse your course? Mountains, why do you skip like rams And hills why do you jump like lambs? You are beholding the face of your Creator, Before God, before the God of Jacob, Turning rocks into swirling waters and stone into a flowing spring.

בְּצֵאת יִשְׂרָאֵל מִמִּצְרָיִם בֵּית יַעֲקֹב מֵעַם לֹעֵז. הָיְתָה יְהוּדָה לְקָדְשׁוֹ יִשְׂרָאֵל מַמְשְׁלוֹתָיו. הַיָּם רָאָה וַיָּנֹס הַיַּרְדֵּן יִסֹּב לְאָחוֹר. הֶהָרִים רָקְדוּ כְאֵילִים גְּבָעוֹת כִּבְנֵי צֹאן. מַה לְּךָ הַיָּם כִּי תָנוּס הַיַּרְדֵּן תִּסֹּב לְאָחוֹר. הֶהָרִים תִּרְקְדוּ כְאֵילִים גְּבָעוֹת כִּבְנֵי צֹאן. מִלִּפְנֵי אָדוֹן חוּלִי אָרֶץ מִלִּפְנֵי אֱלוֹהַּ יַעֲקֹב. הַהֹפְכִי הַצּוּר אֲגַם מָיִם חַלָּמִישׁ לְמַעְיְנוֹ מָיִם.

Blessed are You, Lord, our God, Ruler of the universe, who has redeemed us and our ancestors from Egypt and enabled us to reach this night that we may eat matzah and maror. Lord our God and God of our ancestors, enable us likewise to reach the future holidays and festivals in peace, rejoicing in the rebuilding of Zion your city, and joyful at your service. There we shall eat of the offerings and Passover sacrifices which will be acceptably placed upon your altar. We shall sing a new hymn of praise to you for our redemption and for the liberation of our soul. Blessed are You, Lord, who has redeemed Israel.

Blessed are You, Lord, our God, Ruler of the universe, who has created the fruit of the vine.

We drink the wine immediately, while seated and reclining on the left side.

בָּרוּךְ אַתָּה יְיָ אֱלֹהֵינוּ מֶלֶךְ הָעוֹלָם, אֲשֶׁר גְּאָלָנוּ וְגָאַל אֶת אֲבוֹתֵינוּ מִמִּצְרַיִם, וְהִגִּיעָנוּ הַלַּיְלָה הַזֶּה לֶאֱכָל בּוֹ מַצָּה וּמָרוֹר. כֵּן יְיָ אֱלֹהֵינוּ וֵאלֹהֵי אֲבוֹתֵינוּ יַגִּיעֵנוּ לְמוֹעֲדִים וְלִרְגָלִים אֲחֵרִים הַבָּאִים לִקְרָאתֵנוּ לְשָׁלוֹם, שְׂמֵחִים בְּבִנְיַן עִירֶךְ וְשָׂשִׂים בַּעֲבוֹדָתֶךְ. וְנֹאכַל שָׁם מִן הַזְּבָחִים וּמִן הַפְּסָחִים אֲשֶׁר יַגִּיעַ דָּמָם עַל קִיר מִזְבַּחֲךָ לְרָצוֹן, וְנוֹדֶה לְךָ שִׁיר חָדָשׁ עַל גְּאֻלָתֵנוּ וְעַל פְּדוּת נַפְשֵׁנוּ. בָּרוּךְ אַתָּה יְיָ גָּאַל יִשְׂרָאֵל.

בָּרוּךְ אַתָּה יְיָ אֱלֹהֵינוּ מֶלֶךְ הָעוֹלָם בּוֹרֵא פְּרִי הַגָּפֶן.

רָחְצָה-RAHTZAH

We wash our hands and recite the blessing. Except for the blessings, we do not speak until we have eaten the Matzah. We try to avoid extraneous conversation until Matzah, Marror and Korekh have all been completed.

Blessed are You Lord our God, Ruler of the universe, who has sanctified us with His commandments, and commanded us to wash our hands.

בָּרוּךְ אַתָּה יְיָ אֱלֹהֵינוּ מֶלֶךְ הָעוֹלָם, אֲשֶׁר קִדְּשָׁנוּ בְּמִצְוֹתָיו וְצִוָּנוּ עַל נְטִילַת יָדָיִם.

מוֹצִיא מַצָּה
MOTZI-MATZAH

All three matzot are raised and the first blessing is recited.

Blessed are You Lord our God, Ruler of the universe, who who brings forth bread from the earth.

בָּרוּךְ אַתָּה יְיָ אֱלֹהֵינוּ מֶלֶךְ הָעוֹלָם הַמּוֹצִיא לֶחֶם מִן הָאָרֶץ.

Before eating the matzah, put the bottom matzah back in its place and continue, reciting the following blessing while holding only the top and middle piece of matzah:

Blessed are You Lord our God, Ruler of the universe, who has sanctified us with His commandments, and commanded us to eat matzah.

בָּרוּךְ אַתָּה יְיָ אֱלֹהֵינוּ מֶלֶךְ הָעוֹלָם, אֲשֶׁר קִדְּשָׁנוּ בְּמִצְוֹתָיו וְצִוָּנוּ עַל אֲכִילַת מַצָּה.

Break the top and middle matzot into pieces and distribute them to everyone at the table to eat a while reclining to the left. Additional matzah should be available. Each person should make sure to eat a substantial amount in order to fulfill the mitzvah of eating matzah on this night.

MATZAH AND HUBRIS

The Exodus story and the Harry Potter saga are both tales of the dangers of arrogance and the triumph of humility. Pharaoh's arrogant "Who is God?" needed to be punctured by the plagues, which began, "Through this you shall know that I am God." Pharaoh, who counted himself as one of Egypt's deities, too clever to be defeated by the likes of Moses, "the humblest of men," needed to see all the symbols of his power—the Nile, his sorcery, and his glib tongue—crumble before his eyes. Voldemort considered himself a braver wizard than Dumbledore for venturing into the sinister realm of horcruxes to stave off death. Harry responded, "He

was cleverer than you. A better man. A better wizard." Voldemort's hubris led him to believe that he was the only one who had discovered the Room of Requirement.

The symbol of humility on Pesach is the matzah, which silently urges us to reject the puffery of self-promotion and the emptiness of bloated expansion. In Harry's case, the lesson is conveyed by his ordinary wand of holly, which might not have had the flash of the Elder Wand, but felt so much better in his hand.

MAROR-מָרוֹר

Now take a kezayit (about one ounce) of the maror. Dip it into the Haroset, but not so much that the bitter taste is neutralized. Recite the following blessing and then eat the maror (without reclining):

Blessed are You Lord our God, Ruler of the universe, who has sanctified us with His commandments, and commanded us to eat the bitter herb.

בָּרוּךְ אַתָּה יְיָ אֱלֹהֵינוּ מֶלֶךְ הָעוֹלָם, אֲשֶׁר קִדְּשָׁנוּ בְּמִצְוֹתָיו וְצִוָּנוּ עַל אֲכִילַת מָרוֹר.

KOREKH - כּוֹרֵךְ

Make a sandwich with matzah and maror dipped in haroset and say the following before eating it:

Eating matzah, maror and haroset this way reminds us of how, in the days of the Temple, Hillel would do so, making a sandwich of the Pashal lamb, matzah and maror, in order to observe the law "You shall eat it (the Pesach sacrifice) on matzah and maror."

זֵכֶר לְמִקְדָּשׁ כְּהִלֵּל. כֵּן עָשָׂה הִלֵּל בִּזְמַן שֶׁבֵּית הַמִּקְדָּשׁ הָיָה קַיָּם: הָיָה כּוֹרֵךְ פֶּסַח מַצָּה וּמָרוֹר וְאוֹכֵל בְּיַחַד, לְקַיֵּם מַה שֶׁנֶּאֱמַר: עַל מַצּוֹת וּמְרֹרִים יֹאכְלֻהוּ.

FROM ONE SANDWICH TO ANOTHER

The *Korekh* sandwich recalls how the sage Hillel used to combine the symbols of the Seder and consume them together. This certainly fits with the theme, developed above regarding *Maror*, of the need to see the bitterness of life in context. *Korekh* adds that good must be contextualized, as well, and we must never allow ourselves to get carried away with good fortune that may be fleeting. Life must be accepted on its own terms.

As wizarding fortune would have it, the Harry Potter saga in sandwiched between...two sandwiches. The first, which we will return to in our discussion of wealth, is the dry sandwich that Ron happily abandons in the Hogwarts Express to help Harry consume the goodies he bought from the candy trolley. And after the Battle of Hogwarts is finally over, what does Harry fantasize about but the sandwich that Kreacher might make for him and deliver to Gryffindor Tower.

שֻׁלְחָן עוֹרֵךְ
SHULHAN OREKH

Now is time to enjoy the festival meal and participate in lively discussion. It is permitted to drink wine between the second and third cups. After the meal, take the Afikoman and divide it among all the guests at the Seder table. If the children have gotten hold of it, you may have to offer them an incentive to return it so the Seder can be concluded.

Student Voices - מתלמידי יותר מכולם

Name one way food plays a role in your religious life.

★ Chicken soup ★ Challah ★ Making Berakhot (blessings) ★ Keeping Kosher
★ The "simanim" (symbolic foods, like apple and honey) eaten on Rosh Hashanah. *(Avner, grade 8)*
★ Sufganiyot (jelly donuts eaten on Hanukkah). *(Alex W, grade 5)*

TZAFUN-צָפוּן

We try to avoid drinking or eating anything (except the remaining two ritual cups of wine) after eating the Afikoman.

BAREKH-בָּרֵךְ

Pour the third cup of wine and recite Birkat Hamazon (Grace after the Meal).

A Song of Ascents: When the Lord returns the exiles of Zion, we will be as dreamers. We will laugh and sing with joy. It shall be said among the nations: "The Lord has done great things for them." The Lord did great things for us, and we shall rejoice. God, restore our fortunes so that we shall be like streams in the Negev. Those who sow in tears shall reap in joy. Though the farmer bears the measure of seed to the field in sadness, he shall come home with joy, bearing his sheaves.

שִׁיר הַמַּעֲלוֹת בְּשׁוּב יְיָ אֶת שִׁיבַת צִיּוֹן הָיִינוּ כְּחֹלְמִים. אָז יִמָּלֵא שְׂחוֹק פִּינוּ וּלְשׁוֹנֵנוּ רִנָּה אָז יֹאמְרוּ בַגּוֹיִם הִגְדִּיל יְיָ לַעֲשׂוֹת עִם אֵלֶּה. הִגְדִּיל יְיָ לַעֲשׂוֹת עִמָּנוּ הָיִינוּ שְׂמֵחִים. שׁוּבָה יְיָ אֶת שְׁבִיתֵנוּ כַּאֲפִיקִים בַּנֶּגֶב. הַזֹּרְעִים בְּדִמְעָה בְּרִנָּה יִקְצֹרוּ. הָלוֹךְ יֵלֵךְ וּבָכֹה נֹשֵׂא מֶשֶׁךְ הַזָּרַע בֹּא יָבֹא בְרִנָּה נֹשֵׂא אֲלֻמֹּתָיו.

Leader: Friends, let us say grace.
Participants: Blessed be the name of the Lord now and forever.
Leader: Blessed be the name of the Lord now and forever.
With your permission, let us now bless (our God) whose food we have eaten.
Participants: Blessed be (our God) whose food we have eaten, and through whose goodness we live.
Leader: Blessed be (our God) whose food we have eaten, and through whose goodness we live.

Blessed are You Lord our God, Ruler of the universe, who feeds the whole world in His goodness, with favor, kindness, and mercy. He supplies sustenance to all creatures for His kindness endures forever. And through His great goodness we have never lacked – and may we never lack – sustenance. For the sake of His great name, for he, the Lord, feeds and sustains all, bestowing good upon and preparing food for all the creatures He created Blessed are You Lord who feeds all.

שְׁלֹשָׁה שֶׁאָכְלוּ כְּאֶחָד חַיָבִין
לְזַמֵן וְהַמְזַמֵן פּוֹתֵחַ:
רַבּוֹתַי, נְבָרֵךְ!
הַמְסֻבִּים עוֹנִים: יְהִי שֵׁם יְיָ מְבֹרָךְ
מֵעַתָּה וְעַד עוֹלָם.
הַמְזַמֵן אוֹמֵר: בִּרְשׁוּת מָרָנָן וְרַבָּנָן
וְרַבּוֹתַי, נְבָרֵךְ (בעשרה אֱלֹהֵינוּ)
שֶׁאָכַלְנוּ מִשֶּׁלוֹ.
הַמְסֻבִּים עוֹנִים: בָּרוּךְ (אֱלֹהֵינוּ)
שֶׁאָכַלְנוּ מִשֶּׁלוֹ וּבְטוּבוֹ חָיִינוּ.
הַמְזַמֵן חוֹזֵר וְאוֹמֵר: בָּרוּךְ
(אֱלֹהֵינוּ) שֶׁאָכַלְנוּ מִשֶּׁלוֹ וּבְטוּבוֹ
חָיִינוּ.

בָּרוּךְ אַתָּה יְיָ אֱלֹהֵינוּ מֶלֶךְ
הָעוֹלָם, הַזָּן אֶת הָעוֹלָם כֻּלוֹ
בְּטוּבוֹ בְּחֵן בְּחֶסֶד וּבְרַחֲמִים,
הוּא נֹתֵן לֶחֶם לְכָל-בָּשָׂר כִּי
לְעוֹלָם חַסְדּוֹ, וּבְטוּבוֹ הַגָּדוֹל
תָּמִיד לֹא חָסַר לָנוּ וְאַל יֶחְסַר
לָנוּ מָזוֹן לְעוֹלָם וָעֶד, בַּעֲבוּר
שְׁמוֹ הַגָּדוֹל, כִּי הוּא אֵל זָן
וּמְפַרְנֵס לַכֹּל, וּמֵטִיב לַכֹּל וּמֵכִין
מָזוֹן לְכָל-בְּרִיּוֹתָיו אֲשֶׁר בָּרָא.
בָּרוּךְ אַתָּה יְיָ הַזָּן אֶת הַכֹּל.

We thank you Lord our
God, for having given our
ancestors a beautiful, good, and
spacious land; for having taken
us out from the land of Egypt
and redeemed us from the
house of slavery; for Your
covenant which You sealed
in our flesh; for Your Torah
which You taught us; for Your
laws which You made known to
us; for the life, grace and kindness You have lavished upon us;
and for the food with which You
feed and sustain us always - each
day and each hour.

For everything, Lord our
God, we thank and bless
You. May your name be
blessed by all forever, as it
is written: "After you have
eaten and are satisfied, you
shall bless the Lord, your God
for the good land he has given
you." Blessed are You Lord for
the land and the food.

נוֹדֶה לְךָ יְיָ אֱלֹהֵינוּ עַל
שֶׁהִנְחַלְתָּ לַאֲבוֹתֵינוּ אֶרֶץ
חֶמְדָּה טוֹבָה וּרְחָבָה, וְעַל
שֶׁהוֹצֵאתָנוּ יְיָ אֱלֹהֵינוּ
מֵאֶרֶץ מִצְרַיִם וּפְדִיתָנוּ
מִבֵּית עֲבָדִים, וְעַל בְּרִיתְךָ
שֶׁחָתַמְתָּ בִּבְשָׂרֵנוּ וְעַל
תוֹרָתְךָ שֶׁלִּמַּדְתָּנוּ וְעַל חֻקֶּיךָ
שֶׁהוֹדַעְתָּנוּ, וְעַל חַיִּים חֵן
וָחֶסֶד שֶׁחוֹנַנְתָּנוּ, וְעַל אֲכִילַת
מָזוֹן שָׁאַתָּה זָן וּמְפַרְנֵס
אוֹתָנוּ תָּמִיד, בְּכָל יוֹם וּבְכָל
עֵת וּבְכָל שָׁעָה.

וְעַל הַכֹּל יְיָ אֱלֹהֵינוּ אֲנַחְנוּ
מוֹדִים לָךְ וּמְבָרְכִים אוֹתָךְ,
יִתְבָּרַךְ שִׁמְךָ בְּפִי כָּל חַי תָּמִיד
לְעוֹלָם וָעֶד, כַּכָּתוּב: "וְאָכַלְתָּ
וְשָׂבַעְתָּ, וּבֵרַכְתָּ אֶת יְיָ אֱלֹהֶיךָ
עַל הָאָרֶץ הַטּוֹבָה אֲשֶׁר נָתַן
לָךְ". בָּרוּךְ אַתָּה יְיָ, עַל הָאָרֶץ
וְעַל הַמָּזוֹן.

Have mercy, Lord our God, on Israel your people, on Jerusalem your city, on Zion the abode of your glory, on the kingdom of the house of David your anointed one, and on the great and holy Temple that bears your name. Our God, our Father, tend and feed us; sustain and support us and relieve us. Speedily, Lord our God, grant us relief from all our troubles. Lord our God, please make us not rely on the gifts and loans of men but rather on your full, open, holy, and generous hand, that we may never be put to shame and disgrace.

On Shabbat add:

Favor us and strengthen us, Lord our God, with your commandments – with the commandment concerning the seventh day, this great and holy Sabbath. This day is great and holy before you to abstain from work and rest on it in love according to your will. In your will, Lord our God, grant us rest so that there be no trouble, sorrow or grief on our day of rest. Let us, Lord our God, live to see Zion your city comforted, Jerusalem your holy city rebuilt, for you art Master of all salvation and consolation.)

רַחֶם נָא יְיָ אֱלֹהֵינוּ עַל יִשְׂרָאֵל עַמֶּךָ, וְעַל יְרוּשָׁלַיִם עִירֶךָ, וְעַל צִיּוֹן מִשְׁכַּן כְּבוֹדֶךָ וְעַל מַלְכוּת בֵּית דָּוִד מְשִׁיחֶךָ, וְעַל הַבַּיִת הַגָּדוֹל וְהַקָּדוֹשׁ שֶׁנִּקְרָא שִׁמְךָ עָלָיו. אֱלֹהֵינוּ, אָבִינוּ, רְעֵנוּ, זוּנֵנוּ, פַּרְנְסֵנוּ וְכַלְכְּלֵנוּ וְהַרְוִיחֵנוּ, וְהַרְוַח לָנוּ יְיָ אֱלֹהֵינוּ מְהֵרָה מִכָּל צָרוֹתֵינוּ. וְנָא אַל תַּצְרִיכֵנוּ יְיָ אֱלֹהֵינוּ, לֹא לִידֵי מַתְּנַת בָּשָׂר וָדָם וְלֹא לִידֵי הַלְוָאָתָם, כִּי אִם לְיָדְךָ הַמְּלֵאָה הַפְּתוּחָה הַקְּדוֹשָׁה וְהָרְחָבָה, שֶׁלֹּא נֵבוֹשׁ וְלֹא נִכָּלֵם לְעוֹלָם וָעֶד.

בְּשַׁבָּת מוֹסִיפִין:

רְצֵה וְהַחֲלִיצֵנוּ יְיָ אֱלֹהֵינוּ בְּמִצְוֹתֶיךָ וּבְמִצְוַת יוֹם הַשְּׁבִיעִי הַשַּׁבָּת הַגָּדוֹל וְהַקָּדוֹשׁ הַזֶּה. כִּי יוֹם זֶה גָּדוֹל וְקָדוֹשׁ הוּא לְפָנֶיךָ לִשְׁבָּת בּוֹ וְלָנוּחַ בּוֹ בְּאַהֲבָה כְּמִצְוַת רְצוֹנֶךָ. וּבִרְצוֹנְךָ הָנִיחַ לָנוּ יְיָ אֱלֹהֵינוּ שֶׁלֹּא תְהֵא צָרָה וְיָגוֹן וַאֲנָחָה בְּיוֹם מְנוּחָתֵנוּ. וְהַרְאֵנוּ יְיָ אֱלֹהֵינוּ בְּנֶחָמַת צִיּוֹן עִירֶךָ וּבְבִנְיַן יְרוּשָׁלַיִם עִיר קָדְשֶׁךָ כִּי אַתָּה הוּא בַּעַל הַיְשׁוּעוֹת וּבַעַל הַנֶּחָמוֹת.

God and God of our fathers,
may the remembrance of us,
of our fathers, of the anointed
son of David your servant, of
Jerusalem your holy city, and
of all your people the house of
Israel, ascend, come, appear, be
heard, and be accepted before
you for deliverance and good,
for grace, kindness and mercy,
for life and peace, on this day of
the Festival of Matzot. Remember us this day, Lord our God,
for goodness; consider us for
blessing; save us for life. With
a word of salvation and mercy
spare us and favor us; have pity
on us and save us, for we look
to you, for you art a gracious
and merciful God and King.

Rebuild Jerusalem the holy city
speedily in our days. Blessed are
You, Lord, who will rebuild
Jerusalem in mercy. Amen.

אֱלֹהֵינוּ וֵאלֹהֵי אֲבוֹתֵינוּ, יַעֲלֶה
וְיָבֹא וְיַגִּיעַ, וְיֵרָאֶה וְיֵרָצֶה
וְיִשָּׁמַע, וְיִפָּקֵד וְיִזָּכֵר זִכְרוֹנֵנוּ
וּפִקְדוֹנֵנוּ וְזִכְרוֹן אֲבוֹתֵינוּ,
וְזִכְרוֹן מָשִׁיחַ בֶּן דָּוִד עַבְדֶּךָ,
וְזִכְרוֹן יְרוּשָׁלַיִם עִיר קָדְשֶׁךָ,
וְזִכְרוֹן כָּל עַמְּךָ בֵּית יִשְׂרָאֵל
לְפָנֶיךָ לִפְלֵטָה, לְטוֹבָה, לְחֵן
וּלְחֶסֶד וּלְרַחֲמִים, לְחַיִּים
בְּיוֹם חַג הַמַּצּוֹת הַזֶּה.
זָכְרֵנוּ יְיָ אֱלֹהֵינוּ בּוֹ לְטוֹבָה,
וּפָקְדֵנוּ בוֹ לִבְרָכָה, וְהוֹשִׁיעֵנוּ
בוֹ לְחַיִּים וּבִדְבַר יְשׁוּעָה
וְרַחֲמִים חוּס וְחָנֵּנוּ, וְרַחֵם
עָלֵינוּ וְהוֹשִׁיעֵנוּ, כִּי אֵלֶיךָ
עֵינֵינוּ, כִּי אֵל מֶלֶךְ חַנּוּן
וְרַחוּם אָתָּה.

וּבְנֵה יְרוּשָׁלַיִם עִיר הַקֹּדֶשׁ
בִּמְהֵרָה בְיָמֵינוּ. בָּרוּךְ אַתָּה יְיָ,
בּוֹנֵה בְרַחֲמָיו יְרוּשָׁלָיִם. אָמֵן.

Blessed are You, Lord our God, Ruler of the universe. The God who is our father, our king and sovereign, our creator, our redeemer, our maker, our holy one, the holy one of Jacob, our shepherd, shepherd of Israel, the good king who does good to all and has done good, is doing good, and will do good for us. He bestows favors on us constantly. He lavishes on us grace, kindness and mercy, relief and deliverance, success, blessing, salvation, comfort, sustenance, support, mercy, life and peace and all goodness. May he never deprive us of any good thing.

May the Merciful One reign over us forever and ever. May the Merciful One be blessed in heaven and on earth. May the Merciful One be praised for all generations; may He be glorified in us forever and ever; may He be honored in us to all eternity.

בָּרוּךְ אַתָּה יְיָ, אֱלֹהֵינוּ מֶלֶךְ הָעוֹלָם, הָאֵל אָבִינוּ, מַלְכֵּנוּ, אַדִּירֵנוּ, בּוֹרְאֵנוּ, גֹּאֲלֵנוּ, יוֹצְרֵנוּ, קְדוֹשֵׁנוּ קְדוֹשׁ יַעֲקֹב, רוֹעֵנוּ רוֹעֵה יִשְׂרָאֵל, הַמֶּלֶךְ הַטּוֹב וְהַמֵּטִיב לַכֹּל, שֶׁבְּכָל יוֹם וָיוֹם הוּא הֵטִיב, הוּא מֵטִיב, הוּא יֵיטִיב לָנוּ. הוּא גְמָלָנוּ הוּא גוֹמְלֵנוּ הוּא יִגְמְלֵנוּ לָעַד, לְחֵן וּלְחֶסֶד וּלְרַחֲמִים וּלְרֶוַח הַצָּלָה וְהַצְלָחָה, בְּרָכָה וִישׁוּעָה נֶחָמָה פַּרְנָסָה וְכַלְכָּלָה, וְרַחֲמִים וְחַיִּים וְשָׁלוֹם וְכָל טוֹב; וּמִכָּל טוֹב לְעוֹלָם אַל יְחַסְּרֵנוּ.

הָרַחֲמָן הוּא יִמְלוֹךְ עָלֵינוּ לְעוֹלָם וָעֶד. הָרַחֲמָן הוּא יִתְבָּרַךְ בַּשָּׁמַיִם וּבָאָרֶץ. הָרַחֲמָן הוּא יִשְׁתַּבַּח לְדוֹר דּוֹרִים, וְיִתְפָּאַר בָּנוּ לָעַד וּלְנֵצַח נְצָחִים, וְיִתְהַדַּר בָּנוּ לָעַד וּלְעוֹלְמֵי עוֹלָמִים.

May the Merciful One grant us an honorable livelihood. May the Merciful One break the yoke from our neck; may He lead us upstanding into our land. May the Merciful One send ample blessing into this house and upon this table at which we have eaten. May the Merciful One send us Elijah the prophet of blessed memory who will bring us good tidings of consolation and comfort.

May the Merciful One bless...
If eating at one's parent's home:
...(my revered father) the master of this house and (my revered mother) the mistress of this house, them, and their house-hold, and their children, and everything that is theirs,
If eating at one's own home:
...me (and my wife/husband/chil-dren) and all that is mine,
If one is a guest:
...our host and our hostess, and everything that is theirs,

הָרַחֲמָן הוּא יְפַרְנְסֵנוּ בְּכָבוֹד. הָרַחֲמָן הוּא יִשְׁבּוֹר עֻלֵּנוּ מֵעַל צַוָּארֵנוּ, וְהוּא יוֹלִיכֵנוּ קוֹמְמִיּוּת לְאַרְצֵנוּ. הָרַחֲמָן הוּא יִשְׁלַח לָנוּ בְּרָכָה מְרֻבָּה בַּבַּיִת הַזֶּה, וְעַל שֻׁלְחָן זֶה שֶׁאָכַלְנוּ עָלָיו. הָרַחֲמָן הוּא יִשְׁלַח לָנוּ אֶת אֵלִיָּהוּ הַנָּבִיא זָכוּר לַטּוֹב, וִיבַשֶּׂר לָנוּ בְּשׂוֹרוֹת טוֹבוֹת יְשׁוּעוֹת וְנֶחָמוֹת.

בבית אביו אומר: הָרַחֲמָן הוּא יְבָרֵךְ אֶת אָבִי מוֹרִי בַּעַל הַבַּיִת הַזֶּה, וְאֶת אִמִּי מוֹרָתִי בַּעֲלַת הַבַּיִת הַזֶּה. אוֹתָם וְאֶת בֵּיתָם וְאֶת זַרְעָם וְאֶת כָּל אֲשֶׁר לָהֶם,

נשוי אומר: הָרַחֲמָן הוּא יְבָרֵךְ אוֹתִי, וְאֶת אָבִי מוֹרִי, וְאֶת אִמִּי מוֹרָתִי, וְאֶת אִשְׁתִּי/ וְאֶת בַּעֲלִי, וְאֶת זַרְעִי, וְאֶת כָּל אֲשֶׁר לִי.

אורח אומר: הָרַחֲמָן הוּא יְבָרֵךְ אֶת בַּעַל הַבַּיִת הַזֶּה וְאֶת בַּעֲלַת הַבַּיִת הַזֶּה, אוֹתָם וְאֶת בֵּיתָם וְאֶת זַרְעָם וְאֶת כָּל אֲשֶׁר לָהֶם.

All Continue:

us all together and all our possessions just as He blessed our forefathers Abraham, Isaac, and Jacob,
with every blessing. May He bless
us all together with a perfect blessing, and let us say, Amen.

May heaven find merit in us that
we may enjoy a lasting peace. May
we receive blessings from the Lord,
justice from the God of our salvation,
and may we find favor and good
sense in the eyes of God and men.

On Shabbat:

May the Merciful One cause us to inherit
the day which will be all Sabbath and rest
in the eternal life.

May the Merciful One cause us to
inherit the day of total goodness.
May the Merciful One enable us
to live in the days of the Messiah
and in the world to come. God is
our tower of salvation, showing
kindness to his anointed, to David
and his descendents forever.

May he who creates
peace in his heavenly
heights, may he
grant peace for us,
all Israel; and we
can say, Amen.

אוֹתָנוּ וְאֶת כָּל אֲשֶׁר לָנוּ, כְּמוֹ
שֶׁנִּתְבָּרְכוּ אֲבוֹתֵינוּ אַבְרָהָם
יִצְחָק וְיַעֲקֹב "בַּכֹּל"-"מִכֹּל"-
"כֹּל" – כֵּן יְבָרֵךְ אוֹתָנוּ כֻּלָּנוּ
יַחַד בִּבְרָכָה שְׁלֵמָה. וְנֹאמַר:
"אָמֵן".

בַּמָּרוֹם יְלַמְּדוּ עֲלֵיהֶם וְעָלֵינוּ
זְכוּת שֶׁתְּהֵא לְמִשְׁמֶרֶת שָׁלוֹם.
וְנִשָּׂא בְרָכָה מֵאֵת יְיָ, וּצְדָקָה
מֵאֱלֹהֵי יִשְׁעֵנוּ, וְנִמְצָא חֵן וְשֵׂכֶל
טוֹב בְּעֵינֵי אֱלֹהִים וְאָדָם.

בשבת: הָרַחֲמָן הוּא יַנְחִילֵנוּ יוֹם
שֶׁכֻּלּוֹ שַׁבָּת וּמְנוּחָה לְחַיֵּי הָעוֹלָמִים.

הָרַחֲמָן הוּא יַנְחִילֵנוּ יוֹם שֶׁכֻּלּוֹ
טוֹב. הָרַחֲמָן הוּא יְזַכֵּנוּ לִימוֹת
הַמָּשִׁיחַ וּלְחַיֵּי הָעוֹלָם הַבָּא.

מִגְדּוֹל יְשׁוּעוֹת מַלְכּוֹ, וְעֹשֶׂה
חֶסֶד לִמְשִׁיחוֹ, לְדָוִד וּלְזַרְעוֹ עַד
עוֹלָם.

עֹשֶׂה שָׁלוֹם בִּמְרוֹמָיו, הוּא
יַעֲשֶׂה שָׁלוֹם עָלֵינוּ וְעַל כָּל
יִשְׂרָאֵל. וְאִמְרוּ: "אָמֵן".

Revere the Lord, you His holy ones, for those who revere Him suffer no want. Lions may be famishing and starving, but those who seek the Lord shall not lack any good thing. Give thanks to the Lord, for He is good; his kindness endures forever. You open your hand and satisfy the desire of every living thing. Blessed is the man who trusts in the Lord, and the Lord is his stronghold. I have been young and now I am old, but never have I seen the righteous man forsaken, nor his children wanting bread. The Lord will give strength to his people; the Lord will bless His people with peace.

Raise the cup and recite the blessing.

Blessed are You Lord our God Ruler of the universe, who has created the fruit of the vine.
We drink the wine.

יְראוּ אֶת יְיָ קְדֹשָׁיו, כִּי אֵין מַחְסוֹר לִירֵאָיו. כְּפִירִים רָשׁוּ וְרָעֵבוּ, וְדֹרְשֵׁי יְיָ לֹא יַחְסְרוּ כָל טוֹב. הוֹדוּ לַיְיָ כִּי טוֹב, כִּי לְעוֹלָם חַסְדּוֹ. פּוֹתֵחַ אֶת יָדֶךָ, וּמַשְׂבִּיעַ לְכָל חַי רָצוֹן. בָּרוּךְ הַגֶּבֶר אֲשֶׁר יִבְטַח בַּיְיָ, וְהָיָה יְיָ מִבְטַחוֹ. נַעַר הָיִיתִי גַּם זָקַנְתִּי, וְלֹא רָאִיתִי צַדִּיק נֶעֱזָב, וְזַרְעוֹ מְבַקֶּשׁ לָחֶם. יְיָ עֹז לְעַמּוֹ יִתֵּן, יְיָ יְבָרֵךְ אֶת עַמּוֹ בַשָּׁלוֹם.

בָּרוּךְ אַתָּה יְיָ אֱלֹהֵינוּ מֶלֶךְ הָעוֹלָם בּוֹרֵא פְּרִי הַגָּפֶן.

The fourth cup is filled. An extra cup is filled in honor of Elijah the Prophet. Thr front door of the house is opened to show that Pesach is a night when God protects us against danger.

Pour out your fury on the nations that do not know you, upon the kingdoms that do not invoke your name, for they have devoured Jacob and desolated his home. Pour out your wrath on them; may your blazing anger overtake them. Pursue them in wrath and destroy them from under the heavens of the Lord!

שְׁפֹךְ חֲמָתְךָ אֶל הַגּוֹיִם אֲשֶׁר לֹא יְדָעוּךָ וְעַל מַמְלָכוֹת אֲשֶׁר בְּשִׁמְךָ לֹא קָרָאוּ. כִּי אָכַל אֶת יַעֲקֹב וְאֶת נָוֵהוּ הֵשַׁמּוּ. שְׁפֹךְ עֲלֵיהֶם זַעְמֶךָ וַחֲרוֹן אַפְּךָ יַשִּׂיגֵם. תִּרְדֹּף בְּאַף וְתַשְׁמִידֵם מִתַּחַת שְׁמֵי יְיָ.

WHAT IS ON THE OTHER SIDE OF THE DOOR

Opening the door on the night of the Seder is a symbol of unaccustomed security. On this night, *Leil Shimurim*, the night when God watches over us, we are not afraid of what is on the other side of the door, trying to get at us. During the year, and during long centuries of Jewish history, a knock on the door could be cause for uncertainty, even fear. What physical or spiritual threats want to penetrate our charmed environment and cause us harm? What should we let in and what should we bar? And what opportunities do we miss because we are too fearful to answer the knock? The Song of Songs (*Shir HaShirim*) tells of the knock of the beloved seeking to arouse the maiden, while she is too late in answering. God often knocks when we are too fearful to answer. The Dursleys fled to an isolated island to avoid answering the knock of a world they distrusted. Fortunately for Harry and for us, they did not succeed.

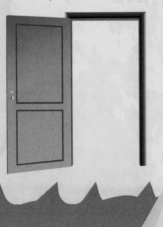

HALLEL-הַלֵּל

Not for us, Lord, not for us, but for Your name bring glory, for the sake of Your kindness and your faithfulness. Why should the nations say: "Where is their God?" Our God is in the heavens; all that He wills, He accomplishes. Their idols are silver and gold, the work of human hands. They have mouths but cannot speak, eyes, but they cannot see, ears but they cannot hear, a nose, but they cannot smell, hands but they cannot feel, feet but they cannot walk; they can utter no sound with their throats. Those who fashion them, whoever trusts in them, shall become like them. Israel, trust in the Lord! He is their help and shield. House of Aaron, trust in the Lord! He is their help and shield. Those who fear the Lord, trust in Him! He is their help and shield.

לֹא לָנוּ יְיָ לֹא לָנוּ, כִּי לְשִׁמְךָ תֵּן כָּבוֹד, עַל חַסְדְּךָ, עַל אֲמִתֶּךָ. לָמָּה יֹאמְרוּ הַגּוֹיִם אַיֵּה נָא אֱלֹהֵיהֶם, וֵאלֹהֵינוּ בַשָּׁמָיִם, כֹּל אֲשֶׁר חָפֵץ עָשָׂה. עֲצַבֵּיהֶם כֶּסֶף וְזָהָב מַעֲשֵׂה יְדֵי אָדָם. פֶּה לָהֶם וְלֹא יְדַבֵּרוּ, עֵינַיִם לָהֶם וְלֹא יִרְאוּ. אָזְנַיִם לָהֶם וְלֹא יִשְׁמָעוּ, אַף לָהֶם וְלֹא יְרִיחוּן. יְדֵיהֶם וְלֹא יְמִישׁוּן, רַגְלֵיהֶם וְלֹא יְהַלֵּכוּ, לֹא יֶהְגּוּ בִּגְרוֹנָם. כְּמוֹהֶם יִהְיוּ עֹשֵׂיהֶם, כֹּל אֲשֶׁר בֹּטֵחַ בָּהֶם. יִשְׂרָאֵל בְּטַח בַּיְיָ, עֶזְרָם וּמָגִנָּם הוּא. בֵּית אַהֲרֹן בִּטְחוּ בַיְיָ, עֶזְרָם וּמָגִנָּם הוּא. יִרְאֵי יְיָ בִּטְחוּ בַיְיָ, עֶזְרָם וּמָגִנָּם הוּא.

The Lord is mindful of us and will bless us; He will bless the house of Israel; He will bless the house of Aaron; He will bless those who fear the Lord, small and great. May the Lord bless you and increase you, you and your children. You are blessed by the Lord, Maker of heaven and earth. The heaven is the Lord's, but He has given the earth to mankind. The dead cannot praise the Lord, nor can any who go down into silence. We will bless the Lord now and forever. Halleluyah.

I love that the Lord. He hears my pleas because He has inclined His ear to me whenever I call. The bonds of death encompassed me, the torments of the grave have overtaken me; I found trouble and sorrow. Then I called upon the name of the Lord: "Please, Lord, save my life!" The Lord is gracious and righteous and our God is merciful. The Lord protects the simple; I was brought low and God saved me. Be at rest, my soul, for the Lord

יְיָ זְכָרָנוּ יְבָרֵךְ, יְבָרֵךְ אֶת בֵּית יִשְׂרָאֵל, יְבָרֵךְ אֶת בֵּית אַהֲרֹן. יְבָרֵךְ יִרְאֵי יְיָ, הַקְּטַנִּים עִם הַגְּדֹלִים. יֹסֵף יְיָ עֲלֵיכֶם, עֲלֵיכֶם וְעַל בְּנֵיכֶם. בְּרוּכִים אַתֶּם לַיְיָ, עֹשֵׂה שָׁמַיִם וָאָרֶץ. הַשָּׁמַיִם שָׁמַיִם לַיְיָ וְהָאָרֶץ נָתַן לִבְנֵי אָדָם. לֹא הַמֵּתִים יְהַלְלוּ יָהּ וְלֹא כָּל יֹרְדֵי דוּמָה. וַאֲנַחְנוּ נְבָרֵךְ יָהּ מֵעַתָּה וְעַד עוֹלָם. הַלְלוּיָהּ:

אָהַבְתִּי כִּי יִשְׁמַע יְיָ אֶת קוֹלִי, תַּחֲנוּנָי. כִּי הִטָּה אָזְנוֹ לִי וּבְיָמַי אֶקְרָא. אֲפָפוּנִי חֶבְלֵי מָוֶת וּמְצָרֵי שְׁאוֹל מְצָאוּנִי, צָרָה וְיָגוֹן אֶמְצָא. וּבְשֵׁם יְיָ אֶקְרָא, אָנָּא יְיָ מַלְּטָה נַפְשִׁי. חַנּוּן יְיָ וְצַדִּיק, וֵאלֹהֵינוּ מְרַחֵם. שֹׁמֵר פְּתָאִים יְיָ, דַּלּוֹתִי וְלִי יְהוֹשִׁיעַ. שׁוּבִי נַפְשִׁי לִמְנוּחָיְכִי, כִּי יְיָ גָּמַל עָלָיְכִי. כִּי חִלַּצְתָּ נַפְשִׁי מִמָּוֶת, אֶת עֵינִי מִן דִּמְעָה, אֶת רַגְלִי מִדֶּחִי. אֶתְהַלֵּךְ לִפְנֵי יְיָ בְּאַרְצוֹת הַחַיִּים. הֶאֱמַנְתִּי

has been good to you. You delivered me from death, my eyes from tears and my feet from stumbling. I shall walk before the Lord in the lands of the living. I trusted even when I spoke out – I was much afflicted. I said in my haste, "All men are false."

כִּי אֲדַבֵּר, אֲנִי עָנִיתִי מְאֹד. אֲנִי אָמַרְתִּי בְחָפְזִי, כָּל הָאָדָם כֹּזֵב.

KOL HA-ADAM KOZEV
CAN PEOPLE BE TRUSTED?

Hallel contains an amalgamation of contradictory feelings. Celebration borders trepidation; thanksgiving alternates with pleading and confidence with fear. Today's victory leaves us looking around the corner for tomorrow's danger. And in one of the Psalmist's lowest moments he confesses, "I said in my haste, 'All men are liars.'" Is it true? In the light of day, after the nightmare-ridden night, does it still seem unwise to trust? King David, the primary author of the Psalms, may have been thinking of episodes in his life when he penned that phrase. When King Saul whose challenger—Goliath—he vanquished turned on him, and when the city of Ke'ila, whom he rescued from attack, informed on him, he surely had a right to doubt the loyalty of human nature. And yet, he qualifies the statement, explaining that it was uttered in a moment of haste, and does not reflect reality.

Probably the best vignette of the resilience of trust is a moment in the life of Luna Lovegood. The night of the final banquet, Harry finds her waiting patiently for all those who had made off with her possessions to return them. He marvels at her attitude. Harry himself shows us that even in an atmosphere where danger lurks, it is possible to find and keep trustworthy friends. He seems to have followed the suggestion of one student who said that you can trust someone who sees you through both good and bad times—he bonded with Hermione as a result of facing a troll together.

?   **Student Voices -** מתלמידי יותר מכולם

When have you felt the most that God cares about you?

★ When I got something I prayed for ★ When I got good grades.

★ When I had a full recovery from a broken arm. *(Gabe S., grade 8)*

★ When I got my dog. *(Ella W., grade 6)*

★ When my GGF lived to 98 through many surgeries. *(Zahava K., grade 6)*

★ When I was saved after having been pulled into the ocean when my dad and my canoe flipped over. *(Daniel S., grade 6)*

★ When I recovered from cancer. *(Cara L., grade 8)*

★ After my surgery. *(Alex W., grade 5)*

★When my brother lost something and I said the Shema and he found it.

How can I repay the Lord for all His kindness to me? I raise the cup of deliverance, and call upon the name of the Lord. My vows to the Lord I pay in the presence of all His people. Precious in the eyes of the Lord is the death of his righteous ones. Please, Lord, I am your servant, your servant, the child of your maid-servant; You have released my bonds. I sacrifice a thanksgiving offering to You, and call upon the name of the Lord. I pay my vows to the Lord in the presence of all God's people, in the courts of the Lord's house, in the midst of Jerusalem. Halleluyah.

מָה אָשִׁיב לַייָ כָּל תַּגְמוּלוֹהִי עָלָי. כּוֹס יְשׁוּעוֹת אֶשָּׂא וּבְשֵׁם יְיָ אֶקְרָא. נְדָרַי לַייָ אֲשַׁלֵּם נֶגְדָה נָּא לְכָל עַמּוֹ. יָקָר בְּעֵינֵי יְיָ הַמָּוְתָה לַחֲסִידָיו. אָנָּא יְיָ כִּי אֲנִי עַבְדֶּךָ, אֲנִי עַבְדְּךָ בֶּן אֲמָתֶךָ, פִּתַּחְתָּ לְמוֹסֵרָי. לְךָ אֶזְבַּח זֶבַח תּוֹדָה וּבְשֵׁם יְיָ אֶקְרָא. נְדָרַי לַייָ אֲשַׁלֵּם נֶגְדָה נָּא לְכָל עַמּוֹ. בְּחַצְרוֹת בֵּית יְיָ, בְּתוֹכֵכִי יְרוּשָׁלָיִם, הַלְלוּיָהּ:

YAKAR B'EINEI HASHEM
PRECIOUS IN GOD'S EYES

As he stumbled from Dumbledore's office, numbed by what he had seen in the Pensieve, Harry knew that he had to die. But worse than that, he knew that he had never mattered. It had only been the plan. He had not been a beloved student of Dumbledore, only a cog in his plan, retained until the

ideal moment of his deployment—and death—to ensure the destruction of Voldemort. He went anyway, but if only he could have walked on to the Forbidden Forest out of a sense of love, rather than responsibility. All he wanted was to know that he mattered to Dumbledore.

This is the feeling captured—and countered—by the Hallel. In the celebratory chapter acknowledging our indebtedness to God, King David declares that, in fact, "Precious in the eyes of God is the death of his righteous ones." At different times in our national history, Jews have been called upon to march to their death. They have not be granted an understanding of God's plan. But they have been able to hold onto the feeling of God's love and the conviction that their death has meaning.

Praise the Lord, all you nations; praise God, all you peoples, for His love to us is great, and the truth of the Lord is forever. Halleluyah.

הַלְלוּ אֶת יְיָ כָּל גּוֹיִם, שַׁבְּחוּהוּ כָּל הָאֻמִּים. כִּי גָבַר עָלֵינוּ חַסְדּוֹ, וֶאֱמֶת יְיָ לְעוֹלָם, הַלְלוּיָהּ:

Give thanks to the Lord, for God is good; His kindness endures forever. Let Israel declare, His kindness endures forever. Let the house of Aaron declare His kindness endures forever. Let those who fear the Lord say His kindness endures forever.

הוֹדוּ לַיְיָ כִּי טוֹב כִּי לְעוֹלָם חַסְדּוֹ.

יֹאמַר נָא יִשְׂרָאֵל כִּי לְעוֹלָם חַסְדּוֹ.

יֹאמְרוּ נָא בֵית אַהֲרֹן כִּי לְעוֹלָם חַסְדּוֹ.

יֹאמְרוּ נָא יִרְאֵי יְיָ כִּי לְעוֹלָם חַסְדּוֹ.

KI L'OLAM CHASDO
HIS KINDNESS ENDURES FOREVER

﹩

According to the Kabbalists, the creation of the world was an act of love. God, the embodiment of goodness, wanted to find a way to bestow good upon others and so He "contracted" Himself to allow for the presence of humans, and set into motion a world in which they could earn their way to His presence. It is God's kindness which animates the world to this day.

All of the events related in the seven Harry Potter novels were set into motion by Lily Potter's one act of kindness and self-sacrifice, in giving her life for Harry. But her act was far from a one-time phenomenon. As we have mentioned and will yet explore, it was the seminal act that paved the way for Harry to follow her example in the end, and to live long enough to do so.

From dire straights I called to the Lord; God answered me with expansiveness. The Lord is with me, I have no fear, what can man do to me? The Lord is with me as my helper, I will see the defeat of all my foes. It is better to take refuge in the Lord than to trust

מִן הַמֵּצַר קָרָאתִי יָּה, עָנָנִי בַּמֶּרְחָב יָה. יְיָ לִי לֹא אִירָא, מַה יַּעֲשֶׂה לִי אָדָם. יְיָ לִי בְּעֹזְרָי וַאֲנִי אֶרְאֶה בְשֹׂנְאָי. טוֹב לַחֲסוֹת בַּיְיָ מִבְּטֹחַ בָּאָדָם. טוֹב לַחֲסוֹת בַּיְיָ מִבְּטֹחַ בִּנְדִיבִים. כָּל גּוֹיִם סְבָבוּנִי, בְּשֵׁם יְיָ כִּי אֲמִילַם.

in man. It is better to take refuge in the Lord than to trust in wealthy people. All nations have surrounded me; in the name of the Lord, I have cut them down. They have repeatedly surround- ed me, in the name of the Lord, I cut them down. They swarmed like bees about me, but they were extinguished like a fire of thorns; but in the name of the Lord, I cut them down. You pushed me and I nearly fell, but the Lord helped me. The Lord is my strength and song; He has become my salvation. The voice of rejoicing and salvation is tents of the righteous resound, "The right hand of the Lord is triumphant! The right hand of the Lord is exalted! The right hand of the Lord triumphs!" I shall not die, but live to proclaim the works of the Lord. The Lord has severely punished me, but he has not handed me over to die. Open the gates of righteousness, that I may enter and praise the Lord. This is the gateway to the Lord, the righteous shall enter through it.

סַבּוּנִי גַם סְבָבוּנִי, בְּשֵׁם יְיָ כִּי אֲמִילַם. סַבּוּנִי כִדְבֹרִים, דֹּעֲכוּ כְּאֵשׁ קוֹצִים, בְּשֵׁם יְיָ כִּי אֲמִילַם. דָּחֹה דְחִיתַנִי לִנְפֹּל, וַיְיָ עֲזָרָנִי. עָזִּי וְזִמְרָת יָהּ וַיְהִי לִי לִישׁוּעָה. קוֹל רִנָּה וִישׁוּעָה בְּאָהֳלֵי צַדִּיקִים, יְמִין יְיָ עֹשָׂה חָיִל. יְמִין יְיָ רוֹמֵמָה, יְמִין יְיָ עֹשָׂה חָיִל. לֹא אָמוּת כִּי אֶחְיֶה, וַאֲסַפֵּר מַעֲשֵׂי יָהּ. יַסֹּר יִסְּרַנִי יָּהּ, וְלַמָּוֶת לֹא נְתָנָנִי. פִּתְחוּ לִי שַׁעֲרֵי צֶדֶק, אָבֹא בָם, אוֹדֶה יָהּ. זֶה הַשַּׁעַר לַיְיָ, צַדִּיקִים יָבֹאוּ בוֹ. אוֹדְךָ כִּי עֲנִיתָנִי וַתְּהִי לִי לִישׁוּעָה. אוֹדְךָ כִּי עֲנִיתָנִי וַתְּהִי לִי לִישׁוּעָה. אֶבֶן מָאֲסוּ הַבּוֹנִים הָיְתָה לְרֹאשׁ פִּנָּה. אֶבֶן מָאֲסוּ הַבּוֹנִים הָיְתָה לְרֹאשׁ פִּנָּה. מֵאֵת יְיָ הָיְתָה זֹּאת הִיא נִפְלָאת בְּעֵינֵינוּ. מֵאֵת יְיָ הָיְתָה זֹּאת הִיא נִפְלָאת בְּעֵינֵינוּ. זֶה הַיּוֹם עָשָׂה יְיָ נָגִילָה וְנִשְׂמְחָה בוֹ. זֶה הַיּוֹם עָשָׂה יְיָ נָגִילָה וְנִשְׂמְחָה בוֹ.

I thank You for though you afflicted me, you have become my salvation. The stone which the builders rejected has become the major cornerstone. This the Lord's doing; it is marvelous in our sight. This is the day, which the Lord has made – let us be glad and rejoice on it.

ODEKHA KI ANITANI
THANK YOU FOR THE AFFLICTION?

There are two ways to translate the verse beginning "*Odekha*," depending upon how you render the word *ki*, which has numerous meanings in scripture. One translation would be, "I thank you— although you afflicted me, you were my salvation." This follows the opinion in medieval grammarians that *ki* can mean "although." The verse does not claim to know what the significance of the affliction was, but thanks God for the deliverance. A second possibility is even more intriguing: "I thank you because you afflicted me and became my salvation." If *ki* denotes the reason for thanking God, the verse is claiming that we must thank God even for the afflictions He brings upon us, because without them, the salvation and growth could never have occurred. The afflictions were necessary to bring us to the next level. Using this approach, one can answer the classic question of why we thank God for taking us out of Egypt when it was He himself who put us there in the first place. In retrospect we see that our right to the land of Israel and the type of people we have become would have been impossible without the experience of servitude in Egypt. Empathy for the oppressed, openness to the other,

abhorrence of slavery and so much more would have been only superficial but for our time in Egypt.

Most of the time, we do not see clearly the benefit that our travails bring us. But J.K. Rowling can do in literature what we cannot do in life—explain everything in the end and justify the suffering that was indispensable in making the final victory possible. The scenes at the end of Book Seven, in "Kings Cross Station" and in the showdown between Harry and Voldemort, answer almost all of the questions in our minds, as they seek, in the words of the 18th century poet Alexander Pope, "To justify the ways of God to man."

Please, Lord, save us!	אָנָּא יְיָ, הוֹשִׁיעָה נָּא.
Please, Lord, save us!	אָנָּא יְיָ, הוֹשִׁיעָה נָּא.
Please, Lord, help us prosper!	אָנָּא יְיָ, הַצְלִיחָה נָא.
Please, Lord, help us prosper!	אָנָּא יְיָ, הַצְלִיחָה נָא.

Blessed be he who comes in the name of the Lord; we bless you from the House of the Lord. The Lord is God, Who has shown us light; bind the festival offering with cords, up to the altar-horns. You are my God, and I thank you; my God, and I exalt you. Give thanks to the Lord, for God is good, His kindness endures forever.

בָּרוּךְ הַבָּא בְּשֵׁם יְיָ, בֵּרַכְנוּכֶם מִבֵּית יְיָ. בָּרוּךְ הַבָּא בְּשֵׁם יְיָ, בֵּרַכְנוּכֶם מִבֵּית יְיָ. אֵל יְיָ וַיָּאֶר לָנוּ. אִסְרוּ חַג בַּעֲבֹתִים עַד קַרְנוֹת הַמִּזְבֵּחַ. אֵל יְיָ וַיָּאֶר לָנוּ. אִסְרוּ חַג בַּעֲבֹתִים עַד קַרְנוֹת הַמִּזְבֵּחַ. אֵלִי אַתָּה וְאוֹדֶךָ, אֱלֹהַי אֲרוֹמְמֶךָּ. אֵלִי אַתָּה וְאוֹדֶךָ, אֱלֹהַי אֲרוֹמְמֶךָּ. הוֹדוּ לַיְיָ כִּי טוֹב, כִּי לְעוֹלָם חַסְדּוֹ. הוֹדוּ לַיְיָ כִּי טוֹב, כִּי לְעוֹלָם חַסְדּוֹ.

Everything that You made will
praise You, God. Your most
righteous people, who do your
will, and all of Your nation, the
family of Israel with glad song will
thank, bless, praise, glorify, exalt,
extol, and sanctify Your name, our
King. For it is good to thank You
and proper to serenade Your name,
because from this world to the
next, You are God forever.

Give thanks to the Lord, for God
is good, for His mercy endures
forever.
Give thanks to the God of gods,
for His mercy endures forever.
Give thanks to the Lord of lords,
for His mercy endures forever.
To the one who does great
wonders, for His mercy endures
forever.
To the one who made the heavens with understanding, for His
mercy endures forever.
To the one that spread forth the
earth above the waters, for His
mercy endures forever.
To the one who made great
luminaries, for His mercy
endures forever;

יְהַלְלוּךְ יי אֱלֹהֵינוּ כָּל מַעֲשֶׂיךָ,
וַחֲסִידֶיךָ צַדִּיקִים עוֹשֵׂי רְצוֹנֶךָ,
וְכָל עַמְּךָ בֵּית יִשְׂרָאֵל בְּרִנָּה
יוֹדוּ וִיבָרְכוּ, וִישַׁבְּחוּ וִיפָאֲרוּ,
וִירוֹמְמוּ וְיַעֲרִיצוּ, וְיַקְדִּישׁוּ
וְיַמְלִיכוּ אֶת שִׁמְךָ, מַלְכֵּנוּ. כִּי
לְךָ טוֹב לְהוֹדוֹת וּלְשִׁמְךָ נָאֶה
לְזַמֵּר, כִּי מֵעוֹלָם וְעַד עוֹלָם
אַתָּה אֵל.

הוֹדוּ לַיי כִּי טוֹב,
כִּי לְעוֹלָם חַסְדּוֹ.
הוֹדוּ לֵאלֹהֵי, הָאֱלֹהִים
כִּי לְעוֹלָם חַסְדּוֹ.
הוֹדוּ לַאֲדֹנֵי הָאֲדֹנִים,
כִּי לְעוֹלָם חַסְדּוֹ
לְעֹשֵׂה נִפְלָאוֹת גְּדֹלוֹת לְבַדּוֹ, כִּי
לְעוֹלָם חַסְדּוֹ
לְעֹשֵׂה הַשָּׁמַיִם בִּתְבוּנָה,
כִּי לְעוֹלָם חַסְדּוֹ
לְרוֹקַע הָאָרֶץ עַל הַמָּיִם,
כִּי לְעוֹלָם חַסְדּוֹ
לְעֹשֵׂה אוֹרִים גְּדֹלִים,
כִּי לְעוֹלָם חַסְדּוֹ

The sun to reign by day, for His mercy endures forever;	אֶת הַשֶּׁמֶשׁ לְמֶמְשֶׁלֶת בַּיּוֹם, כִּי לְעוֹלָם חַסְדּוֹ
The moon and stars to reign by night, for His mercy endures forever.	אֶת הַיָּרֵחַ וְכוֹכָבִים לְמֶמְשְׁלוֹת בַּלָּיְלָה - כִּי לְעוֹלָם חַסְדּוֹ
To the one who smote great kings; for His mercy endures forever;	לְמַכֵּה מִצְרַיִם בִּבְכוֹרֵיהֶם, כִּי לְעוֹלָם חַסְדּוֹ
And took Israel out from among them, for His mercy endures forever;	וַיּוֹצֵא יִשְׂרָאֵל מִתּוֹכָם, כִּי לְעוֹלָם חַסְדּוֹ
With a strong hand and an outstretched arm, for His mercy endures forever.	בְּיָד חֲזָקָה וּבִזְרוֹעַ נְטוּיָה, כִּי לְעוֹלָם חַסְדּוֹ
To Him who parted the Red Sea, for His mercy endures forever;	לְגֹזֵר יַם סוּף לִגְזָרִים, כִּי לְעוֹלָם חַסְדּוֹ
And made Israel to pass through it, for His mercy endures for-ever;	וְהֶעֱבִיר יִשְׂרָאֵל בְּתוֹכוֹ, כִּי לְעוֹלָם חַסְדּוֹ
And threw Pharaoh and his host in the Red Sea, for His mercy endures forever.	וְנִעֵר פַּרְעֹה וְחֵילוֹ בְיַם סוּף, כִּי לְעוֹלָם חַסְדּוֹ
To Him who led His people through the wilderness, for His mercy endures forever.	לְמוֹלִיךְ עַמּוֹ בַּמִּדְבָּר, כִּי לְעוֹלָם חַסְדּוֹ
To Him who smote great kings; for His mercy endures forever;	לְמַכֵּה מְלָכִים גְּדֹלִים, כִּי לְעוֹלָם חַסְדּוֹ
And slew mighty kings, for His mercy endures forever.	וַיַּהֲרֹג מְלָכִים אַדִּירִים, כִּי לְעוֹלָם חַסְדּוֹ

Sihon, King of the Emorites, for
His mercy endures forever;
And Og, King of Bashan, for
His mercy endures forever;
And gave their land as an inheritance, for His mercy endures
forever;
An inheritance for Israel His
servant, for His mercy endures
forever.
Who remembered us in our
low state, for His mercy endures
forever;
And delivered us from our ad-
versaries, for His mercy endures
forever.
Who gives food to all creatures,
for His mercy endures forever.
Give thanks to the God of
heaven, for His mercy endures
forever.

The soul of every living being shall
bless your name, Lord our God the
spirit of all flesh shall ever glorify
and exalt your remembrance,
our King. Through-
out eternity Thou
art God. Besides
You we have no
king

לְסִיחוֹן מֶלֶךְ הָאֱמֹרִי,
כִּי לְעוֹלָם חַסְדּוֹ

וּלְעוֹג מֶלֶךְ הַבָּשָׁן,
כִּי לְעוֹלָם חַסְדּוֹ

וְנָתַן אַרְצָם לְנַחֲלָה,
כִּי לְעוֹלָם חַסְדּוֹ

נַחֲלָה לְיִשְׂרָאֵל עַבְדּוֹ,
כִּי לְעוֹלָם חַסְדּוֹ

שֶׁבְּשִׁפְלֵנוּ זָכַר לָנוּ,
כִּי לְעוֹלָם חַסְדּוֹ

וַיִּפְרְקֵנוּ מִצָּרֵינוּ,
כִּי לְעוֹלָם חַסְדּוֹ

נֹתֵן לֶחֶם לְכָל בָּשָׂר,
כִּי לְעוֹלָם חַסְדּוֹ

הוֹדוּ לְאֵל הַשָּׁמָיִם,
כִּי לְעוֹלָם חַסְדּוֹ:

נִשְׁמַת כָּל חַי תְּבָרֵךְ אֶת שִׁמְךָ
יְיָ אֱלֹהֵינוּ, וְרוּחַ כָּל בָּשָׂר תְּפָאֵר
וּתְרוֹמֵם זִכְרְךָ מַלְכֵּנוּ תָּמִיד.
מִן הָעוֹלָם וְעַד הָעוֹלָם אַתָּה
אֵל, וּמִבַּלְעָדֶיךָ אֵין לָנוּ מֶלֶךְ
גּוֹאֵל וּמוֹשִׁיעַ, פּוֹדֶה וּמַצִּיל

who redeems and saves, ransoms and rescues, sustains and shows mercy in all times of trouble and distress. We have no King but You-God of the first and of the last, God of all creatures, Master of all generations, One acclaimed with a multitude of praises, He who guides His world with kindness and His creatures with mercy. The Lord neither slumbers nor sleeps; He rouses those who sleep and wakens those who slumber; He enables the mute to speak and frees the captive; He supports those who are fallen and raises those who are bowed down. To You alone we give thanks.

Were our mouth filled with song as the ocean, and our tongue with melody as the endless waves; were our lips full of praise as the wide heavens, and our eyes shining like the sun and the moon; were our hands outstretched as the eagles of the sky and our legs as swift as the gazelle--we should still be unable to thank You and bless your name, Lord

וּמְפַרְנֵס וּמְרַחֵם בְּכָל עֵת
צָרָה וְצוּקָה. אֵין לָנוּ מֶלֶךְ
אֶלָּא אָתָּה. אֱלֹהֵי הָרִאשׁוֹנִים
וְהָאַחֲרוֹנִים, אֱלוֹהַּ כָּל בְּרִיּוֹת,
אֲדוֹן כָּל תּוֹלָדוֹת, הַמְהֻלָּל
בְּרֹב הַתִּשְׁבָּחוֹת, הַמְנַהֵג
עוֹלָמוֹ בְּחֶסֶד וּבְרִיּוֹתָיו
בְּרַחֲמִים. וַיְיָ לֹא יָנוּם וְלֹא
יִישָׁן, הַמְעוֹרֵר יְשֵׁנִים וְהַמֵּקִיץ
נִרְדָּמִים, וְהַמֵּשִׂיחַ אִלְּמִים
וְהַמַּתִּיר אֲסוּרִים, וְהַסּוֹמֵךְ
נוֹפְלִים וְהַזּוֹקֵף כְּפוּפִים, לְךָ
לְבַדְּךָ אֲנַחְנוּ מוֹדִים.

אִלּוּ פִינוּ מָלֵא שִׁירָה כַּיָּם,
וּלְשׁוֹנֵנוּ רִנָּה כַּהֲמוֹן גַּלָּיו,
וְשִׂפְתוֹתֵינוּ שֶׁבַח כְּמֶרְחֲבֵי
רָקִיעַ, וְעֵינֵינוּ מְאִירוֹת כַּשֶּׁמֶשׁ
וְכַיָּרֵחַ, וְיָדֵינוּ פְרוּשׂוֹת כְּנִשְׁרֵי
שָׁמַיִם, וְרַגְלֵינוּ קַלּוֹת כָּאַיָּלוֹת,
אֵין אֲנַחְנוּ מַסְפִּיקִים לְהוֹדוֹת
לְךָ, יְיָ אֱלֹהֵינוּ וֵאלֹהֵי אֲבוֹתֵינוּ,
וּלְבָרֵךְ אֶת שְׁמֶךָ, עַל אַחַת
מֵאֶלֶף אַלְפֵי אֲלָפִים וְרִבֵּי
רִבָבוֹת פְּעָמִים

our God and God of our fathers, for one of the thousands and even myriads of favors which You have bestowed on our fathers and on us. You have liberated us from Egypt, Lord our God, and redeemed us from the house of slavery. You have fed us in famine and sustained us with plenty. You have saved us from the sword, helped us to escape the plague, and spared us from severe and enduring diseases. Until now your mercy has helped us, and your kindness has not forsaken us; may You, Lord our God, never abandon us.

Therefore, the limbs which You have given us, the spirit and soul which You have breathed into our nostrils, and the tongue which You have placed in our mouth, shall all thank and bless, praise and glorify, exalt and re- vere, sanctify and acclaim your name, our King. To You, every mouth shall offer thanks; every tongue shall vow allegiance; every knee shall bend, and all who stand erect shall bow. All hearts shall

הַטּוֹבוֹת שֶׁעָשִׂיתָ עִם אֲבוֹתֵינוּ וְעִמָּנוּ. מִמִּצְרַיִם גְּאַלְתָּנוּ, יְיָ אֱלֹהֵינוּ, וּמִבֵּית עֲבָדִים פְּדִיתָנוּ, בְּרָעָב זַנְתָּנוּ וּבְשָׂבָע כִּלְכַּלְתָּנוּ, מֵחֶרֶב הִצַּלְתָּנוּ וּמִדֶּבֶר מִלַּטְתָּנוּ, וּמֵחֳלָיִם רָעִים וְרַבִּים וְנֶאֱמָנִים דִּלִּיתָנוּ. עַד הֵנָּה עֲזָרוּנוּ רַחֲמֶיךָ וְלֹא עֲזָבוּנוּ חֲסָדֶיךָ, וְאַל תִּטְּשֵׁנוּ יְיָ אֱלֹהֵינוּ לָנֶצַח.

עַל כֵּן אֵבָרִים שֶׁפִּלַּגְתָּ בָּנוּ וְרוּחַ וּנְשָׁמָה שֶׁנָּפַחְתָּ בְּאַפֵּינוּ וְלָשׁוֹן אֲשֶׁר שַׂמְתָּ בְּפִינוּ, הֵן הֵם יוֹדוּ וִיבָרְכוּ וִישַׁבְּחוּ וִיפָאֲרוּ וִירוֹמְמוּ וְיַעֲרִיצוּ וְיַקְדִּישׁוּ וְיַמְלִיכוּ אֶת שִׁמְךָ מַלְכֵּנוּ. כִּי כָל פֶּה לְךָ יוֹדֶה, וְכָל לָשׁוֹן לְךָ תִשָּׁבַע, וְכָל בֶּרֶךְ לְךָ תִכְרַע, וְכָל קוֹמָה לְפָנֶיךָ תִשְׁתַּחֲוֶה, וְכָל לְבָבוֹת יִירָאוּךָ, וְכָל קֶרֶב וּכְלָיוֹת יְזַמְּרוּ לִשְׁמֶךָ, כַּדָּבָר שֶׁכָּתוּב, כָּל עַצְמֹתַי תֹּאמַרְנָה: יְיָ, מִי כָמוֹךָ!, מַצִּיל עָנִי מֵחָזָק מִמֶּנּוּ וְעָנִי וְאֶבְיוֹן מִגֹּזְלוֹ.

revere You, and men's inner beings shall sing to your name, as it
is written: "All my bones shall
say: Lord, who is like You?"
You save the poor man from
one who is stronger, the poor
and needy from he that would
rob them. Who may be likened
to You? Who is equal to You?
Who can be compared to You?
Great, mighty and revered
God, supreme God is the Master
of heaven and earth. Let us
praise, acclaim and glorify You
and bless Your holy name, as it
is said: "A Psalm of David: Bless
the Lord, my soul, and let my
whole inner being bless His holy
name." God in your mighty acts
of power, great in the honor of
your name, powerful forever and
revered for your awe-inspiring
acts, O King seated upon a high
and lofty throne!

He who abides forever, exalted
and holy is His name. And it is
written: "Rejoice in the Lord,
you righteous; it is pleasant for
the upright to give praise." By
the mouth of the upright you

מִי יִדְמֶה לָּךְ וּמִי יִשְׁוֶה לָּךְ וּמִי
יַעֲרָךְ לָךְ, הָאֵל הַגָּדוֹל, הַגִּבּוֹר
וְהַנּוֹרָא, אֵל עֶלְיוֹן, קֹנֵה
שָׁמַיִם וָאָרֶץ. נְהַלֶּלְךָ וּנְשַׁבֵּחֲךָ
וּנְפָאֶרְךָ וּנְבָרֵךְ אֶת שֵׁם קָדְשֶׁךָ,
כָּאָמוּר: לְדָוִד, בָּרְכִי נַפְשִׁי אֶת
יְיָ וְכָל קְרָבַי אֶת שֵׁם קָדְשׁוֹ.

הָאֵל בְּתַעֲצֻמוֹת עֻזֶּךָ, הַגָּדוֹל
בִּכְבוֹד שְׁמֶךָ, הַגִּבּוֹר לָנֶצַח
וְהַנּוֹרָא בְּנוֹרְאוֹתֶיךָ, הַמֶּלֶךְ
הַיּוֹשֵׁב עַל כִּסֵּא רָם וְנִשָּׂא.

שׁוֹכֵן עַד מָרוֹם וְקָדוֹשׁ שְׁמוֹ.
וְכָתוּב: רַנְּנוּ צַדִּיקִים בַּיְיָ,
לַיְשָׁרִים נָאוָה תְהִלָּה.
בְּפִי יְשָׁרִים תִּתְהַלָּל,
וּבְדִבְרֵי צַדִּיקִים תִּתְבָּרַךְ,
וּבִלְשׁוֹן חֲסִידִים תִּתְרוֹמָם,
וּבְקֶרֶב קְדוֹשִׁים תִּתְקַדָּשׁ.

וּבְמַקְהֲלוֹת רִבְבוֹת עַמְּךָ בֵּית
יִשְׂרָאֵל בְּרִנָּה יִתְפָּאֵר שִׁמְךָ,
מַלְכֵּנוּ, בְּכָל דּוֹר וָדוֹר. שֶׁכֵּן
חוֹבַת כָּל הַיְצוּרִים, לְפָנֶיךָ יְיָ
אֱלֹהֵינוּ וֵאלֹהֵי אֲבוֹתֵינוּ

shall be praised; By the words of
the righteous you shall be blessed;
By the tongue of the pious you
shall be exalted; And in the midst
of the holy you shall be sanctified.

In the assemblies of the multitudes
of your people, the house of Israel,
with song shall your name,
our King, be glorified in every
generation. For it is the duty of all
creatures to thank, praise, laud,
extol, exalt, adore, and bless Thee;
even beyond the songs and praises
of David the son of Jesse,
your anointed servant.

Praised be your name forever,
our God, our King, who is great
and holy in heaven and on earth;
for to You, Lord our God, it is
fitting to render song and praise,
hymn and psalm, power and
dominion, victory, greatness and
might, paeon and beauty, holiness and sovereignty, blessings
and thanks, from now and
forever.

Blessed are You God, God, King great in praise, God of
thanksgivings, Master of wonders, who desires melodi-
ous songs, King, God, life of the universe.

לְהוֹדוֹת, לְהַלֵּל, לְשַׁבֵּחַ, לְפָאֵר,
לְרוֹמֵם, לְהַדֵּר, לְבָרֵךְ, לְעַלֵּה
וּלְקַלֵּס עַל כָּל דִּבְרֵי שִׁירוֹת
וְתִשְׁבְּחוֹת דָּוִד בֶּן יִשַׁי עַבְדֶּךָ,
מְשִׁיחֶךָ.

יִשְׁתַּבַּח שִׁמְךָ לָעַד מַלְכֵּנוּ,
הָאֵל הַמֶּלֶךְ הַגָּדוֹל וְהַקָּדוֹשׁ
בַּשָּׁמַיִם וּבָאָרֶץ, כִּי לְךָ נָאֶה,
יְיָ אֱלֹהֵינוּ וֵאלֹהֵי אֲבוֹתֵינוּ,
שִׁיר וּשְׁבָחָה, הַלֵּל וְזִמְרָה,
עֹז וּמֶמְשָׁלָה, נֶצַח, גְּדֻלָּה
וּגְבוּרָה, תְּהִלָּה וְתִפְאֶרֶת,
קְדֻשָּׁה וּמַלְכוּת, בְּרָכוֹת
וְהוֹדָאוֹת מֵעַתָּה וְעַד עוֹלָם.
בָּרוּךְ אַתָּה יְיָ, אֵל מֶלֶךְ גָּדוֹל
בַּתִּשְׁבָּחוֹת, אֵל הַהוֹדָאוֹת,
אֲדוֹן הַנִּפְלָאוֹת, הַבּוֹחֵר בְּשִׁירֵי
זִמְרָה, מֶלֶךְ אֵל חֵי הָעוֹלָמִים.

Raise up the cup and recite:

Blessed are You, Lord our God, Ruler of the universe, who has created the fruit of the vine.

בָּרוּךְ אַתָּה יְיָ אֱלֹהֵינוּ מֶלֶךְ הָעוֹלָם בּוֹרֵא פְּרִי הַגָּפֶן.

Drink the fourth cup while leaning. After drinking recite:

Blessed are You Lord our God, Ruler of the universe, for the vine and the fruit, and for produce of the field, for the desirable, beautiful and spacious land, which you desired and gave to our ancestors to eat from its fruit and be sated from its goodness. Have mercy, Lord our God, on Israel Your people, on Jerusalem Your city, on Zion, abode of Your glory, on Your altar and Your sanctuary. Rebuild Jerusalem, the holy city, speedily in our days. Bring us there and cheer us with its restoration; may we eat Israel's produce and enjoy its goodness;

בָּרוּךְ אַתָּה יְיָ אֱלֹהֵינוּ מֶלֶךְ הָעוֹלָם, עַל הַגֶּפֶן וְעַל פְּרִי הַגֶּפֶן, עַל תְּנוּבַת הַשָּׂדֶה וְעַל אֶרֶץ חֶמְדָּה טוֹבָה וּרְחָבָה שֶׁרָצִיתָ וְהִנְחַלְתָּ לַאֲבוֹתֵינוּ לֶאֱכֹל מִפִּרְיָהּ וְלִשְׂבֹּעַ מִטּוּבָהּ רַחֵם נָא ד' אֱלֹקֵינוּ עַל יִשְׂרָאֵל עַמֶּךָ וְעַל יְרוּשָׁלַיִם עִירֶךָ וְעַל צִיּוֹן מִשְׁכַּן כְּבוֹדֶךָ וְעַל מִזְבְּחֶךָ וְעַל הֵיכָלֶךָ וּבְנֵה יְרוּשָׁלַיִם עִיר הַקֹּדֶשׁ בִּמְהֵרָה בְיָמֵינוּ וְהַעֲלֵנוּ לְתוֹכָהּ וְשַׂמְּחֵנוּ בְּבִנְיָנָהּ וְנֹאכַל מִפִּרְיָהּ וְנִשְׂבַּע מִטּוּבָהּ וּנְבָרֶכְךָ עָלֶיהָ בִּקְדֻשָּׁה וּבְטָהֳרָה (בְּשַׁבָּת: וּרְצֵה וְהַחֲלִיצֵנוּ

we shall praise you from upon it with holiness and purity. (On Shabbat add: Favor us and strengthen us on this Sabbath day) and grant us happiness on this Feast of Matzot, For you, Lord, are good and beneficent to all, and we thank you for the land and the fruit of the vine. Blessed are You, Lord, for the land and the fruit of the vine.

בְּיוֹם הַשַׁבָּת הַזֶה) וְשַׂמְּחֵנוּ בְּיוֹם חַג הַמַּצוֹת הַזֶה, כִּי אַתָּה ד' טוֹב וּמֵטִיב לַכֹּל וְנוֹדֶה לְךָ עַל הָאָרֶץ וְעַל פְּרִי הַגָּפֶן. בָּרוּךְ אַתָּה ד' עַל הָאָרֶץ וְעַל פְּרִי הַגָּפֶן.

נִרְצָה-NIRTZAH

The Passover seder has been completed correctly according to all its laws. Just as we merited to have a Passover seder, so may we merit to bring the Passover offering.

Pure One, who dwells in the heavens, Raise up the assembly that cannot be numbered. Bring near the day when You lead the stock that you planted, redeemed, to Zion in joy.

חֲסַל סִדּוּר פֶּסַח כְּהִלְכָתוֹ, כְּכָל מִשְׁפָּטוֹ וְחֻקָתוֹ. כַּאֲשֶׁר זָכִינוּ לְסַדֵּר אוֹתוֹ כֵּן נִזְכֶּה לַעֲשׂוֹתוֹ.

זָךְ שׁוֹכֵן מְעוֹנָה,קוֹמֵם קְהַל עֲדַת מִי מָנָה. בְּקָרוֹב נַהֵל נִטְעֵי כַנָּה, פְּדוּיִם לְצִיוֹן בְּרִנָּה.

לְשָׁנָה הַבָּאָה בִּירוּשָׁלָיִם.

Next year in Jerusalem!

On the first night recite:

It came to pass at Midnight…
You brought about many miracles at night.
At the beginning of the watches on this night
You brought victory to [Abraham,] the righteous convert,
It came to pass at Midnight…
You passed judgment on the king of Gerar in a dream of night
You frightened [Laban] the Aramean "last night."
Israel fought with God and prevailed over him at night.
It came to pass at Midnight…
You crushed the firstborn of Pathros [Egypt] at midnight.
They did not find their host when they rose at night.
You defeated the prince of Harosheth (Sisera) with the stars of night.
It came to pass at Midnight…
You dried up the corpses of the blasphemer [Sennacherib] who plotted to rise up against Zion at night.
[The statue of] Bel and the one who erected it [Nebuchadnezar] kneeled in the dark of night.

וּבְכֵן וַיְהִי בַּחֲצִי הַלַּיְלָה

אָז רוֹב נִסִּים הִפְלֵאתָ בַּלַּיְלָה,
בְּרֹאשׁ אַשְׁמוֹרֶת זֶה הַלַּיְלָה,
גֵּר צֶדֶק נִצַּחְתּוֹ כְּנֶחֱלַק לוֹ לַיְלָה,
וַיְהִי בַּחֲצִי הַלַּיְלָה.

דַּנְתָּ מֶלֶךְ גְּרָר בַּחֲלוֹם הַלַּיְלָה,
הִפְחַדְתָּ אֲרַמִּי בְּאֶמֶשׁ לַיְלָה,
וַיָּשַׂר יִשְׂרָאֵל לְמַלְאָךְ וַיּוּכַל לוֹ
לַיְלָה,
וַיְהִי בַּחֲצִי הַלַּיְלָה.

זֶרַע בְּכוֹרֵי פַתְרוֹס מָחַצְתָּ
בַּחֲצִי הַלַּיְלָה,
חֵילָם לֹא מָצְאוּ בְּקוּמָם
בַּלַּיְלָה,

טִיסַת נְגִיד חֲרֶשֶׁת סִלִּיתָ
בְּכוֹכְבֵי לַיְלָה,
וַיְהִי בַּחֲצִי הַלַּיְלָה.

יָעַץ מְחָרֵף לְנוֹפֵף אִוּוּי, הוֹבַשְׁתָּ
פְגָרָיו בַּלַּיְלָה,
כָּרַע בֵּל וּמַצָּבוֹ בְּאִישׁוֹן לַיְלָה,
לְאִישׁ חֲמוּדוֹת נִגְלָה רָז חֲזוֹת
לַיְלָה,
וַיְהִי בַּחֲצִי הַלַּיְלָה.

The secret of visions was revealed to the beloved man [Daniel] at night.

It came to pass at Midnight…
[Belshazar,] the one who became drunk by [drinking from] the sacred vessels was killed on that night.
[Daniel] was saved from the pit of lions, he who interpreted the terrors of night.
The Aggagite [Haman] nursed his hatred and wrote edicts at night.

It came to pass at Midnight…
You aroused your victory over him [Haman] when sleep fled [from Ahasuerus] at night.
You will trample the winepress for [the one who asks,] "Watchman, what of the night?"
He [God] cried out like a watchman, saying, "Morning has come, as well as Layla/Night.

It came to pass at Midnight…

מִשְׁתַּכֵּר בִּכְלֵי קֹדֶשׁ נֶהֱרַג בּוֹ
בַּלַּיְלָה,
נוֹשַׁע מִבּוֹר אֲרָיוֹת פּוֹתֵר
בִּעֲתוּתֵי לַיְלָה,
שִׂנְאָה נָטַר אֲגָגִי וְכָתַב סְפָרִים
בַּלַּיְלָה,
וַיְהִי בַּחֲצִי הַלַּיְלָה.

עוֹרַרְתָּ נִצְחֲךָ עָלָיו בְּנֶדֶד שְׁנַת
לַיְלָה,
פּוּרָה תִדְרוֹךְ לְשׁוֹמֵר מַה
מִלַּיְלָה,
צָרַח כַּשּׁוֹמֵר וְשָׂח "אָתָא בֹקֶר
וְגַם לַיְלָה",
וַיְהִי בַּחֲצִי הַלַּיְלָה.

קָרֵב יוֹם אֲשֶׁר הוּא לֹא יוֹם
וְלֹא לַיְלָה,
רָם הוֹדַע כִּי לְךָ הַיּוֹם אַף לְךָ
הַלַּיְלָה,
שׁוֹמְרִים הַפְקֵד לְעִירְךָ כָּל הַיּוֹם
וְכָל הַלַּיְלָה,
תָּאִיר כְּאוֹר יוֹם חֶשְׁכַּת לַיְלָה,
וַיְהִי בַּחֲצִי הַלַּיְלָה.

Bring near the day is that is neither day nor night. Most High,
make known that Yours is the day as well as the night.
Appoint watchmen [to guard] Your city all day and all night.
Illuminate like day the dark of night.
It came to pass at Midnight…

On the second night recite:

You shall say: "The Passover sacrifice."
You wrought mighty wonders on Passover.
The first of all the holidays, You exalted Passover.
You revealed to the Ezrahite [Abraham] [that which would occur] at midnight on Passover.
You shall say: "The Passover sacrifice."
You knocked on his [Abraham's] door in the heat of the day on Passover.
He fed the luminous [angels] loaves of matzah on Passover.
He ran to the cattle, which are reminiscent of the ox about which we read on Passover.
You shall say: "The Passover sacrifice."
Your wrath was unleashed on the inhabitants of Sodom, who were

וּבְכֵן וַאֲמַרְתֶּם זֶבַח פֶּסַח

אֹמֶץ גְּבוּרוֹתֶיךָ הִפְלֵאתָ בַּפֶּסַח,
בְּרֹאשׁ כָּל מוֹעֲדוֹת נִשֵּׂאתָ פֶּסַח,
גִּלִּיתָ לְאֶזְרָחִי חֲצוֹת לֵיל פֶּסַח,
וַאֲמַרְתֶּם זֶבַח פֶּסַח.

דְּלָתָיו דָּפַקְתָּ כְּחֹם הַיּוֹם
בַּפֶּסַח, **הִסְעִיד** נוֹצְצִים עֻגוֹת
מַצּוֹת בַּפֶּסַח, **וְאֶל** הַבָּקָר
רָץ זֵכֶר לְשׁוֹר עֵרֶךְ פֶּסַח,
וַאֲמַרְתֶּם זֶבַח פֶּסַח.

זוֹעֲמוּ סְדוֹמִים וְלוֹהֲטוּ בָּאֵשׁ
בַּפֶּסַח, **חֻלַּץ** לוֹט מֵהֶם וּמַצּוֹת
אָפָה בְּקֵץ פֶּסַח, **טִאטֵאתָ**
אַדְמַת מֹף וְנֹף בְּעָבְרְךָ בַּפֶּסַח,
וַאֲמַרְתֶּם זֶבַח פֶּסַח.

יָהּ רֹאשׁ כָּל אוֹן מָחַצְתָּ בְּלֵיל
שִׁמּוּר פֶּסַח, **כַּבִּיר**, עַל בֵּן בְּכוֹר
פָּסַחְתָּ בְּדַם פֶּסַח, **לְבִלְתִּי** תֵּת
מַשְׁחִית לָבֹא בִּפְתָחַי בַּפֶּסַח,
וַאֲמַרְתֶּם זֶבַח פֶּסַח.

burned by fire on Passover. Lot escaped from them and baked matzah at the end of Passover. You destroyed the land of Moph and Noph [Egypt] when you passed through on Passover. **You shall say: "The Passover sacrifice."**

Yah, You crushed the all the first of their strength on the night of the observance of Passover. Mighty One, You passed over the son [Israel] with the blood of the lamb of Passover. So as not to allow the Destroyer to enter my doorways on Passover. **You shall say: "The Passover sacrifice."**

The enclosed [city of Jericho] was closed at the time of Passover. Midian was destroyed by a cake of barley from the omer-offering of Passover. The fat of Pul and Lud [Assyria] was burned by a fire kindled on Passover. **You shall say: "The Passover sacrifice."**

Still on this day, he [Sennacherib] stood at Nob until the arrival of the season of Passover. The hand wrote, engraving deeply, on Passover.

"Let the watchmen watch!" "Set the table!"— on Passover.

You shall say: "The Passover sacrifice."

מִסְגֶּרֶת סֻגְּרָה בְּעִתּוֹתֵי פֶּסַח, נִשְׁמְדָה מִדְיָן בִּצְלִיל שְׂעוֹרֵי עֹמֶר פֶּסַח, **שׂ**וֹרְפוּ מִשְׁמַנֵּי פּוּל וְלוּד בִּיקַד יְקוֹד פֶּסַח, וַאֲמַרְתֶּם זֶבַח פֶּסַח.

עוֹד הַיּוֹם בְּנֹב לַעֲמוֹד עַד גָּעָה עוֹנַת פֶּסַח, **פַּ**ס יַד כָּתְבָה לְקַעֲקֵעַ צוּל בַּפֶּסַח, **צָ**פֹה הַצָּפִית עָרוֹךְ הַשֻּׁלְחָן בַּפֶּסַח, וַאֲמַרְתֶּם זֶבַח פֶּסַח.

קָהָל כִּנְּסָה הֲדַסָּה לְשַׁלֵּשׁ צוֹם בַּפֶּסַח, **ר**ֹאשׁ מִבֵּית רָשָׁע מָחַצְתָּ בְּעֵץ חֲמִשִּׁים בַּפֶּסַח, **שְׁ**תֵּי אֵלֶּה רֶגַע תָּבִיא לְעוּצִית בַּפֶּסַח, **תָּ**עֹז יָדְךָ וְתָרוּם יְמִינְךָ כְּלֵיל הִתְקַדֶּשׁ חַג פֶּסַח, וַאֲמַרְתֶּם זֶבַח פֶּסַח.

Hadassah assembled the people to fast for three days on Passover.
You crushed the roof of the wicked one's [Haman's] house with a
fifty-[cubit] stake on Passover.
Cause these two things to happen to the Utsite [Edom] on Passover.
May Your hand be strengthened, may Your right hand be mightily
exalted, as on the night of the holy festival of Passover.

Because it is proper for Him, because it befits Him.
Mighty in sovereignty, right-ly select. His minions say to Him: "Yours and Yours, Yours because it is Yours, Yours and only Yours— Yours, Lord, is sovereignty!"
Because it is proper for Him, because it befits Him.
Exalted in sovereignty, rightly glorious. His faithful ones say to Him: "Yours and Yours, Yours because it is Yours, Yours and only Yours— Yours, Lord, is sovereignty!"
Because it is proper for Him, because it befits Him.
Blameless in sovereignty, right-ly powerful. His generals say to Him: "Yours and Yours, Yours because it is Yours, Yours and only Yours— Yours, Lord, is sovereignty!"

כִּי לוֹ נָאֶה, כִּי לוֹ יָאֶה

אַדִּיר בִּמְלוּכָה, **בָּחוּר**
כַּהֲלָכָה, **גְּ**דוּדָיו יֹאמְרוּ לוֹ: לְךָ
וּלְךָ, לְךָ כִּי לְךָ, לְךָ אַף לְךָ, לְךָ
יְיָ הַמַּמְלָכָה, כִּי לוֹ נָאֶה, כִּי לוֹ
יָאֶה.

דָּגוּל בִּמְלוּכָה, **הָ**דוּר כַּהֲלָכָה,
וָתִיקָיו יֹאמְרוּ לוֹ: לְךָ וּלְךָ,
לְךָ כִּי לְךָ, לְךָ אַף לְךָ, לְךָ יְיָ
הַמַּמְלָכָה, כִּי לוֹ נָאֶה, כִּי לוֹ
יָאֶה.

זַכַּאי בִּמְלוּכָה, **חָ**סִין כַּהֲלָכָה
טַפְסְרָיו יֹאמְרוּ לוֹ: לְךָ וּלְךָ,
לְךָ כִּי לְךָ, לְךָ אַף לְךָ, לְךָ יְיָ
הַמַּמְלָכָה, כִּי לוֹ נָאֶה, כִּי לוֹ
יָאֶה.

Because it is proper for Him, because it befits Him.
Singular in sovereignty, rightly strong. His learned ones say to Him: "Yours and Yours, Yours because it is Yours, Yours and only Yours— Yours, Lord, is sovereignty!"
Because it is proper for Him, because it befits Him.
Exalted in sovereignty, rightly awesome. Those who surround Him say to Him: "Yours and Yours, Yours because it is Yours, Yours and only Yours— Yours, Lord, is sovereignty!"
Because it is proper for Him, because it befits Him.
Humble in sovereignty, rightly saving. His righteous ones say to Him: "Yours and Yours, Yours because it is Yours, Yours and only Yours— Yours, Lord, is sovereignty!"

יָחִיד בִּמְלוּכָה, **כַּבִּיר** כַּהֲלָכָה **לִמּוּדָיו** יֹאמְרוּ לוֹ: לְךָ וּלְךָ, לְךָ כִּי לְךָ, לְךָ אַף לְךָ, לְךָ יְיָ הַמַּמְלָכָה, כִּי לוֹ נָאֶה, כִּי לוֹ יָאֶה.

מוֹשֵׁל בִּמְלוּכָה, **נוֹרָא** כַּהֲלָכָה **סְבִיבָיו** יֹאמְרוּ לוֹ: לְךָ וּלְךָ, לְךָ כִּי לְךָ, לְךָ אַף לְךָ, לְךָ יְיָ הַמַּמְלָכָה, כִּי לוֹ נָאֶה, כִּי לוֹ יָאֶה.

עָנָיו בִּמְלוּכָה, **פּוֹדֶה** כַּהֲלָכָה, **צַדִּיקָיו** יֹאמְרוּ לוֹ: לְךָ וּלְךָ, לְךָ כִּי לְךָ, לְךָ אַף לְךָ, לְךָ יְיָ הַמַּמְלָכָה, כִּי לוֹ נָאֶה, כִּי לוֹ יָאֶה.

קָדוֹשׁ בִּמְלוּכָה, **רַחוּם** כַּהֲלָכָה **שִׁנְאַנָּיו** יֹאמְרוּ לוֹ: לְךָ וּלְךָ, לְךָ כִּי לְךָ, לְךָ אַף לְךָ, לְךָ יְיָ הַמַּמְלָכָה, כִּי לוֹ נָאֶה, כִּי לוֹ יָאֶה.

תַּקִּיף בִּמְלוּכָה, **תּוֹמֵךְ** כַּהֲלָכָה **תְּמִימָיו** יֹאמְרוּ לוֹ: לְךָ וּלְךָ, לְךָ כִּי לְךָ, לְךָ אַף לְךָ, לְךָ יְיָ הַמַּמְלָכָה, כִּי לוֹ נָאֶה, כִּי לוֹ יָאֶה.

Because it is proper for Him, because it befits Him.
Holy in sovereignty, rightly merciful. His multitudes say to Him:
"Yours and Yours, Yours because it is Yours, Yours and only
Yours— Yours, Lord, is sovereignty!"
Because it is proper for Him, because it befits Him.
Strong in sovereignty, rightly supportive. His perfect ones say
to Him: "Yours and Yours, Yours because it is Yours, Yours and
only Yours— Yours, Lord, is sovereignty!"

He is mighty. May He rebuild
His temple soon! Speedily,
speedily, in our days, soon!
God, build! God, build! Rebuild
Your temple soon!

אַדִּיר הוּא יִבְנֶה בֵּיתוֹ בְּקָרוֹב.
בִּמְהֵרָה, בִּמְהֵרָה, בְּיָמֵינוּ
בְּקָרוֹב. אֵל בְּנֵה, אֵל בְּנֵה,
בְּנֵה בֵיתְךָ בְּקָרוֹב.

He is select. He is great.
He is lofty. May He rebuild
His temple soon! Speedily,
speedily, in our days, soon!
God, build! God, build! Rebuild
Your temple soon!

בָּחוּר הוּא, **גָּדוֹל** הוּא, **דָּגוּל**
הוּא יִבְנֶה בֵּיתוֹ בְּקָרוֹב.
בִּמְהֵרָה, בִּמְהֵרָה, בְּיָמֵינוּ
בְּקָרוֹב. אֵל בְּנֵה, אֵל בְּנֵה,
בְּנֵה בֵיתְךָ בְּקָרוֹב.

He is glorious. He is just. He is
blameless. He is righteous. May
He rebuild His temple soon!
Speedily, speedily, in our days,
soon! God, build! God, build!
Rebuild Your temple soon!

הָדוּר הוּא, **וָתִיק** הוּא, **זַכַּאי**
הוּא, **חָסִיד** הוּא יִבְנֶה בֵּיתוֹ
בְּקָרוֹב. בִּמְהֵרָה, בִּמְהֵרָה,
בְּיָמֵינוּ בְּקָרוֹב. אֵל בְּנֵה, אֵל
בְּנֵה, בְּנֵה בֵיתְךָ בְּקָרוֹב.

He is pure. He is singular.
He is powerful. He is learned.
He is Sovereign. May He re-

טָהוֹר הוּא, יָחִיד הוּא, **כַּבִּיר**
הוּא, **לָמוּד** הוּא, **מֶלֶךְ** הוּא

build His temple soon! Speedily, speedily, in our days, soon! God, build! God, build! Rebuild Your temple soon!

He is awesome He is strong. He is valorous. He is redemptive. He is just.May He rebuild His temple soon! Speedily, speedily in our days, soon! God, build! God, build! Rebuild Your temple soon!

He is holy. He is merciful. He is God. He is commanding. May He rebuild His temple soon! Speedily, speedily, in our days, soon! God, build! God, build! Rebuild Your temple soon!

Who knows one? I know one! One is our God in the heavens and the earth.

Who knows two? I know two! Two are the tablets of the covenant, and one is our God in the heavens and the earth.

יִבְנֶה בֵּיתוֹ בְּקָרוֹב. בִּמְהֵרָה, בִּמְהֵרָה, בְּיָמֵינוּ בְּקָרוֹב. אֵל בְּנֵה, אֵל בְּנֵה, בְּנֵה בֵיתְךָ בְּקָרוֹב.

נוֹרָא הוּא, **ס**גִּיב הוּא, **ע**זּוּז הוּא, **פּ**וֹדֶה הוּא, **צ**דִיק הוּא יִבְנֶה בֵּיתוֹ בְּקָרוֹב. בִּמְהֵרָה, בִּמְהֵרָה, בְּיָמֵינוּ בְּקָרוֹב. אֵל בְּנֵה, אֵל בְּנֵה, בְּנֵה בֵיתְךָ בְּקָרוֹב.

קדוֹשׁ הוּא, **ר**חוּם הוּא, **שַׁ**דַּי הוּא, **תּ**קִיף הוּא יִבְנֶה בֵּיתוֹ בְּקָרוֹב. בִּמְהֵרָה, בִּמְהֵרָה, בְּיָמֵינוּ בְּקָרוֹב. אֵל בְּנֵה, אֵל בְּנֵה, בְּנֵה בֵיתְךָ בְּקָרוֹב.

אֶחָד מִי יוֹדֵעַ, אֶחָד אֲנִי יוֹדֵעַ. אֶחָד אֱלֹהֵינוּ שֶׁבַּשָּׁמַיִם וּבָאָרֶץ:

שְׁנַיִם מִי יוֹדֵעַ, שְׁנַיִם אֲנִי יוֹדֵעַ. שְׁנֵי לֻחוֹת הַבְּרִית. אֶחָד אֱלֹהֵינוּ שֶׁבַּשָּׁמַיִם וּבָאָרֶץ:

Who knows three? I know three! Three are the Patriarchs, two are the tablets of the covenant, and one is our God in the heavens and the earth.

Who knows four? I know four! Four are the matriarchs, three are the patriarchs, two are the tablets of the covenant, and one is our God in the heavens and the earth.

Who knows five? I know five! Five are the books of the Torah, four are the matriarchs, three are the patriarchs, two are the tablets of the covenant, and one is our God in the heavens and the earth.

Who knows six? I know six! Six are the orders of the Mishnah, five are the books of the Torah, four are the matriarchs, three are the patriarchs, two are the tablets of the covenant, and one is our God in the heavens and the earth.

Who knows seven? I know seven! seven are the days of the week, six are the orders of the Mishnah, five are the books of

שְׁלֹשָׁה מִי יוֹדֵעַ, שְׁלֹשָׁה אֲנִי יוֹדֵעַ. שְׁלֹשָׁה אָבוֹת, שְׁנֵי לֻחוֹת הַבְּרִית, אֶחָד אֱלֹהֵינוּ שֶׁבַּשָּׁמַיִם וּבָאָרֶץ:

אַרְבַּע מִי יוֹדֵעַ, אַרְבַּע אֲנִי יוֹדֵעַ. אַרְבַּע אִמָּהוֹת, שְׁלֹשָׁה אָבוֹת, שְׁנֵי לֻחוֹת הַבְּרִית, אֶחָד אֱלֹהֵינוּ שֶׁבַּשָּׁמַיִם וּבָאָרֶץ:

חֲמִשָּׁה מִי יוֹדֵעַ, חֲמִשָּׁה אֲנִי יוֹדֵעַ. חֲמִשָּׁה חֻמְשֵׁי תוֹרָה, אַרְבַּע אִמָּהוֹת, שְׁלֹשָׁה אָבוֹת, שְׁנֵי לֻחוֹת הַבְּרִית, אֶחָד אֱלֹהֵינוּ שֶׁבַּשָּׁמַיִם וּבָאָרֶץ:

שִׁשָּׁה מִי יוֹדֵעַ, שִׁשָּׁה אֲנִי יוֹדֵעַ. שִׁשָּׁה סִדְרֵי מִשְׁנָה, חֲמִשָּׁה חֻמְשֵׁי תוֹרָה, אַרְבַּע אִמָּהוֹת, שְׁלֹשָׁה אָבוֹת, שְׁנֵי לֻחוֹת הַבְּרִית, אֶחָד אֱלֹהֵינוּ שֶׁבַּשָּׁמַיִם וּבָאָרֶץ:

שִׁבְעָה מִי יוֹדֵעַ, שִׁבְעָה אֲנִי יוֹדֵעַ. שִׁבְעָה יְמֵי שַׁבַּתָּא, שִׁשָּׁה סִדְרֵי מִשְׁנָה, חֲמִשָּׁה

the Torah, four are the matriarchs, three are the patriarchs, two are the tablets of the covenant, and one is our God in the heavens and the earth.

Who knows eight? I know eight! Eight are the days until circumcision, seven are the days of the week, six are the orders of the Mishnah, five are the matriarchs, four are the covenant, three are the patriarchs, two are the tablets of the books of the Torah, and one is our God in the heavens and the earth.

Who knows nine? I know nine! Nine are the months of pregnancy, eight are the days until circumcision, seven are the days of the week, six are the orders of the Mishnah, five are the books of the Torah, four are the matriarchs, three are the patriarchs, two are the tablets of the covenant, and one is our God in the heavens and the earth.

חוּמְשֵׁי תוֹרָה, אַרְבַּע אִמָּהוֹת, שְׁלֹשָׁה אָבוֹת, שְׁנֵי לֻחוֹת הַבְּרִית, אֶחָד אֱלֹהֵינוּ שֶׁבַּשָּׁמַיִם וּבָאָרֶץ:

שְׁמוֹנָה מִי יוֹדֵעַ, שְׁמוֹנָה אֲנִי יוֹדֵעַ. שְׁמוֹנָה יְמֵי מִילָה, שִׁבְעָה יְמֵי שַׁבַּתָּא, שִׁשָּׁה סִדְרֵי מִשְׁנָה, חֲמִשָּׁה חוּמְשֵׁי תוֹרָה, אַרְבַּע אִמָּהוֹת, שְׁלֹשָׁה אָבוֹת,שְׁנֵי לֻחוֹת הַבְּרִית, אֶחָד אֱלֹהֵינוּ שֶׁבַּשָּׁמַיִם וּבָאָרֶץ:

תִּשְׁעָה מִי יוֹדֵעַ, תִּשְׁעָה אֲנִי יוֹדֵעַ. תִּשְׁעָה יַרְחֵי לֵדָה, שְׁמוֹנָה יְמֵי מִילָה, שִׁבְעָה יְמֵי שַׁבַּתָּא, שִׁשָּׁה סִדְרֵי מִשְׁנָה, חֲמִשָּׁה חוּמְשֵׁי תוֹרָה, אַרְבַּע אִמָּהוֹת, שְׁלֹשָׁה אָבוֹת, שְׁנֵי לֻחוֹת הַבְּרִית, אֶחָד אֱלֹהֵינוּ שֶׁבַּשָּׁמַיִם וּבָאָרֶץ:

עֲשָׂרָה מִי יוֹדֵעַ, עֲשָׂרָה אֲנִי יוֹדֵעַ. עֲשָׂרָה דִבְּרַיָּא, תִּשְׁעָה יַרְחֵי לֵדָה, שְׁמוֹנָה יְמֵי מִילָה, שִׁבְעָה יְמֵי שַׁבַּתָּא, שִׁשָּׁה סִדְרֵי מִשְׁנָה, חֲמִשָּׁה חוּמְשֵׁי

Who knows ten? I know ten! Ten are the commandments, nine are the months of pregnancy, eight are the days until circumcision, seven are the days of the week, six are the orders of the Mishnah, five are the books of the Torah, four are the matriarchs, three are the patriarchs, two are the tablets of the covenant, and one is our God in the heavens and the earth.

Who knows eleven? I know eleven! Eleven are the stars [in Joseph's dream], ten are the commandments, nine are the months of pregnancy, eight are the days until circumcision, seven are the days of the week, six are the orders of the Mishnah, five are the books of the Torah, four are the matriarchs, three are the patriarchs, two are the tablets of the covenant, and one is our God in the heavens and the earth.

Who knows twelve? I know twelve! Twelve are the tribes [of Israel], eleven are the stars in

תּוֹרָה, אַרְבַּע אִמָּהוֹת, שְׁלֹשָׁה אָבוֹת, שְׁנֵי לֻחוֹת הַבְּרִית, אֶחָד אֱלֹהֵינוּ שֶׁבַּשָּׁמַיִם וּבָאָרֶץ:

אַחַד עָשָׂר מִי יוֹדֵעַ, אַחַד עָשָׂר אֲנִי יוֹדֵעַ. אַחַד עָשָׂר כּוֹכְבַיָּא, עֲשָׂרָה דִבְּרַיָּא, תִּשְׁעָה יַרְחֵי לֵדָה, שְׁמוֹנָה יְמֵי מִילָה, שִׁבְעָה יְמֵי שַׁבַּתָּא, שִׁשָּׁה סִדְרֵי מִשְׁנָה חֲמִשָּׁה חוּמְשֵׁי תוֹרָה, אַרְבַּע אִמָּהוֹת, שְׁלֹשָׁה אָבוֹת, שְׁנֵי לֻחוֹת הַבְּרִית, אֶחָד אֱלֹהֵינוּ שֶׁבַּשָּׁמַיִם וּבָאָרֶץ:

שְׁנֵים עָשָׂר מִי יוֹדֵעַ, שְׁנֵים עָשָׂר אֲנִי יוֹדֵעַ. שְׁנֵים עָשָׂר שִׁבְטַיָּא, אַחַד עָשָׂר כּוֹכְבַיָּא, עֲשָׂרָה דִבְּרַיָּא, תִּשְׁעָה יַרְחֵי לֵדָה, שְׁמוֹנָה יְמֵי מִילָה, שִׁבְעָה יְמֵי שַׁבַּתָּא, שִׁשָּׁה סִדְרֵי מִשְׁנָה, חֲמִשָּׁה חוּמְשֵׁי תוֹרָה, אַרְבַּע אִמָּהוֹת, שְׁלֹשָׁה אָבוֹת, שְׁנֵי לֻחוֹת הַבְּרִית, אֶחָד אֱלֹהֵינוּ שֶׁבַּשָּׁמַיִם וּבָאָרֶץ:

Joseph's dream, ten are the commandments, nine are the months of pregnancy, eight are the days until circumcision, seven are the days of the week, six are the orders of the Mishnah, five are the books of the Torah, four are the matriarchs, three are the patriarchs, two are the tablets of the covenant, and one is our God in the heavens and the earth.

Who knows thirteen? I know thirteen! Thirteen are the attributes [of God's mercy], twelve are the tribes [of Israel], eleven are the stars in Joseph's dream, ten are the commandments, nine are the months of pregnancy, eight are the days until circumcision, seven are the days of the week, six are the orders of the Mishnah, five are the books of the Torah, four are the matriarchs, three are the patriarchs, two are the tablets of the covenant, and one is our God in the heavens and the earth.

שְׁלֹשָׁה עָשָׂר מִי יוֹדֵעַ, שְׁלֹשָׁה עָשָׂר אֲנִי יוֹדֵעַ. שְׁלֹשָׁה עָשָׂר מִדַּיָּא. שְׁנֵים עָשָׂר שִׁבְטַיָּא, אַחַד עָשָׂר כּוֹכְבַיָּא, עֲשָׂרָה דִבְּרַיָּא, תִּשְׁעָה יַרְחֵי לֵדָה, שְׁמוֹנָה יְמֵי מִילָה, שִׁבְעָה יְמֵי שַׁבַּתָּא, שִׁשָּׁה סִדְרֵי מִשְׁנָה, חֲמִשָּׁה חוּמְשֵׁי תוֹרָה, אַרְבַּע אִמָּהוֹת, שְׁלֹשָׁה אָבוֹת, שְׁנֵי לֻחוֹת הַבְּרִית, אֶחָד אֱלֹהֵינוּ שֶׁבַּשָּׁמַיִם וּבָאָרֶץ:

One little **goat**, one little goat that my father bought for two zuzim.

A **cat** came and ate the goat that my father bought for two zuzim. One little goat, one little goat.

חַד גַּדְיָא, חַד גַּדְיָא דְּזַבִּין אַבָּא בִּתְרֵי זוּזֵי, חַד גַּדְיָא, חַד גַּדְיָא. וְאָתָא שׁוּנְרָא וְאָכְלָה לְגַדְיָא, דְּזַבִּין אַבָּא בִּתְרֵי זוּזֵי, חַד גַּדְיָא, חַד גַּדְיָא.

A **dog** came and bit the cat that ate the goat that my father bought for two zuzim. One little goat, one little goat.

A **stick** came and hit the dog that bit the cat that ate the goat that my father bought for two zuzim. One little goat, one little goat.

A **fire** came and burned the stick that hit the dog that bit the cat that ate the goat that my father bought for two zuzim. One little goat, one little goat.

Water came and put out the fire that burned the stick that hit the dog that bit the cat that ate the goat that my father bought for two zuzim. One little goat, one little goat.

An **ox** came and drank the water that put out the fire that burned the stick that hit the dog that bit the cat that ate the goat that my father bought for two zuzim. One little goat, one little goat.

וְאָתָא **כַלְבָּא** וְנָשַׁךְ לְשׁוּנְרָא, דְּאָכְלָה לְגַדְיָא, דְּזַבִּין אַבָּא בִּתְרֵי זוּזֵי, חַד גַּדְיָא, חַד גַּדְיָא.

וְאָתָא **חוּטְרָא** וְהִכָּה לְכַלְבָּא, דְּנָשַׁךְ לְשׁוּנְרָא, דְּאָכְלָה לְגַדְיָא, דְּזַבִּין אַבָּא בִּתְרֵי זוּזֵי, חַד גַּדְיָא, חַד גַּדְיָא..

וְאָתָא **נוּרָא** וְשָׂרַף לְחוּטְרָא, דְּהִכָּה לְכַלְבָּא, דְּנָשַׁךְ לְשׁוּנְרָא, דְּאָכְלָה לְגַדְיָא, דְּזַבִּין אַבָּא בִּתְרֵי זוּזֵי, חַד גַּדְיָא, חַד גַּדְיָא.

וְאָתָא **מַיָּא** וְכָבָה לְנוּרָא, דְּשָׂרַף לְחוּטְרָא, דְּהִכָּה לְכַלְבָּא, דְּנָשַׁךְ לְשׁוּנְרָא, דְּאָכְלָה לְגַדְיָא, דְּזַבִּין אַבָּא בִּתְרֵי זוּזֵי, חַד גַּדְיָא, חַד גַּדְיָא.

וְאָתָא **תּוֹרָא** וְשָׁתָה לְמַיָּא, דְּכָבָה לְנוּרָא, דְּשָׂרַף לְחוּטְרָא, דְּהִכָּה לְכַלְבָּא, דְּנָשַׁךְ לְשׁוּנְרָא, דְּאָכְלָה לְגַדְיָא, דְּזַבִּין אַבָּא בִּתְרֵי זוּזֵי, חַד גַּדְיָא, חַד גַּדְיָא.

A **butcher** came and slaughtered the ox that drank the water that put out the fire that burned the stick that hit the dog that bit the cat that ate the goat that my father bought for two zuzim. One little goat, one little goat.

The **angel of death** came and slaughtered the butcher who slaughtered the ox that drank the water that put out the fire that burned the stick that hit the dog that bit the cat that ate the goat that my father bought for two zuzim. One little goat, one little goat.

Then the **Holy One, Blessed** be He, came and slaughtered the angel of death who slaughtered the butcher who slaughtered the ox that drank the water that put out the fire that burned the stick that hit the dog that bit the cat that ate the goat that my father bought for two zuzim. One little goat, one little goat.

וְאָתָא **הַשּׁוֹחֵט** וְשָׁחַט לְתוֹרָא, דְּשָׁתָה לְמַיָּא, דְּכָבָה לְנוּרָא, דְּשָׂרַף לְחוּטְרָא, דְּהִכָּה לְכַלְבָּא, דְּנָשַׁךְ לְשׁוּנְרָא, דְּאָכְלָה לְגַדְיָא, דְּזַבִּין אַבָּא בִּתְרֵי זוּזֵי, חַד גַּדְיָא, חַד גַּדְיָא.

וְאָתָא **מַלְאַךְ הַמָּוֶת** וְשָׁחַט לְשׁוֹחֵט, דְּשָׁחַט לְתוֹרָא, דְּשָׁתָה לְמַיָּא, דְּכָבָה לְנוּרָא, דְּשָׂרַף לְחוּטְרָא, דְּהִכָּה לְכַלְבָּא, דְּנָשַׁךְ לְשׁוּנְרָא, דְּאָכְלָה לְגַדְיָא, דְּזַבִּין אַבָּא בִּתְרֵי זוּזֵי, חַד גַּדְיָא, חַד גַּדְיָא.

וְאָתָא **הַקָּדוֹשׁ בָּרוּךְ הוּא** וְשָׁחַט לְמַלְאַךְ הַמָּוֶת, דְּשָׁחַט לְשׁוֹחֵט, דְּשָׁחַט לְתוֹרָא, דְּשָׁתָה לְמַיָּא, דְּכָבָה לְנוּרָא, דְּשָׂרַף לְחוּטְרָא, דְּהִכָּה לְכַלְבָּא, דְּנָשַׁךְ לְשׁוּנְרָא, דְּאָכְלָה לְגַדְיָא, דְּזַבִּין אַבָּא בִּתְרֵי זוּזֵי, חַד גַּדְיָא, חַד גַּדְיָא.

UNCONDITIONAL LOVE
GOATS AND CHAIN REACTIONS

⚡

The Seder ends with what appears to be a folk song which traces a chain of events from the purchase of a baby goat, a kid, for two zuzim, through its consumption by a cat, who is bitten by a dog, who is struck by a stick, which is burnt by fire, itself quenched by water, later drunk by an ox who is slaughtered by a butcher, himself dispatched by the angel of death, who is finally vanquished by God. This "simple" ditty has been the subject of numerous interpretations over the generations: The kid represents the Jewish people and the later characters are the ups and downs of Jewish history; or the kid represents Joseph and each stanza is something that happened to him, and so on. But one thing is clear. Every event has a cause, and, in turn, serves as a cause for other events, in a long chain of causation. When we see something remarkable happening, we must realize that it was only possible because of all the stages that preceded it.

By the time Harry Potter duels and defeats Lord Voldemort (spoiler alert?) in the dramatic climax to the whole saga, J.K. Rowling had put into place an extraordinarily complex chain of events, causes and effects, that combined to make his victory possible.

Not only does this remind us to bear in mind how many steps led to the denouement of the Harry Potter books, but we learn how even one rung removed from the ladder, would have made ultimate victory impossible. In our own lives, when it is so easy to rationalize away the need to exercise self discipline on any given day, it would be helpful to remember the lesson of how every step counts.

Perhaps we might phrase some of the steps along the way in a Chad Gadya-esque manner:

I.
Unconditional Love, unconditional love
That Lily showed to sacrifice for Harry
Unconditional love, unconditional love.

II.
Harry's heart wouldn't let him murder Wormtail
Though he betrayed Lily
Whose love had saved her son.
Unconditional love, unconditional love.

III.
Wormtail hesitated and was strangled
'Cause Harry saved his life
Though he betrayed his mom
Whose love had saved her son
Unconditional love, unconditional love

IV.

Harry disarmed Malfoy 'cause Wormtail hesitated
'Cause Harry saved his life
Though he betrayed his mom
Whose love had saved her son
Now Dobby could save all
Cause Harry set him free
Unconditional love, unconditional love.

V.

Malfoy had the wand cause he disarmed poor Albus
'Cause Dumbledore had paused
To look out for Harry
So Harry got it too
When Wormtail's face turned blue
'Cause Harry saved his life
Though he betrayed his mom
Whose love had saved her son
So Dobby could save all
'Cause Harry set him free
Unconditional love, unconditional love

VI.

The Dark Lord was in shock—he never saw it coming
'Cause he had trusted Snape
But Snape loved Lily more
And worked for Dumbledore
Protecting Harry too
Even when he killed his boss
When Dumbledore had paused
And so his wand was lost

Til Harry got it too
When Wormtail's face turned blue
'Cause Harry saved his life
Though he betrayed his mom
Whose love had saved her son
So Dobby could save all
'Cause Harry set him free
Unconditional love, unconditional love.

VII.
Then Harry gave his life to shield his friends and family
Just as Lily had
When dying with his dad
Like mother and like kid
But Riddle didn't see
The love that saved Harry
Now Harry took the stick
On Draco played a trick
Who disarmed Dumbledore
Who paused to help Harry
So Harry got it too
When Wormtail's face turned blue
'Cause Harry saved his life
Though he betrayed his mom
Whose love had saved her son
So Dobby could save all
'Cause Harry set him free
Unconditional love,
unconditional love.

Made in the USA
Middletown, DE
03 April 2017